The Brown Palace Hotel

ABSOLUTELY FIREPROOF

DENVER LITHO. CO.

Denver, Colo, 7/3 191

Mr A E Carlton, Room 516
& Wfe

To The Brown Palace Hotel, Dr.

C. H. Morse, Manager.

For Room	1 Sup	3	9 0
		9	0 0
Cafe 3 25 4 25		7	5 0
	Ex		15
Baggage & Express 2 5 50			75
Livery			
Laundry			
Bar & Wine		1	0 0
Cigars & Papers			
Telegrams & Messengers			
Valet		1	0
Phone 17			8
Bill Rendered			

For

"Welcome Arch" from Union Depot, Denver, Colo.

BROWN PALACE HOTEL BY NIGHT, DENVER, COLO.

THE BROWN PALACE HOTEL

DENVER, COLORADO

The Brown Palace
Denver's Grande Dame

CORINNE HUNT

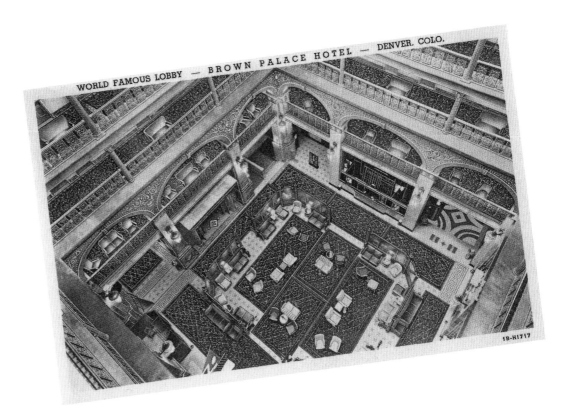

Copyright © 2003
The Brown Palace Hotel
321 Seventeenth Street
Denver, Colorado 80202-4003
www.BrownPalace.com
1-800-321-2599

ISBN 0-9728912-0-X

Julia Kanellos, Hotel Historian, research
Deborah Dix, Hotel Director of Public Relations

Prepared for publication by Archetype Press, Inc.
Diane Maddex, Project Director
Gretchen Smith Mui, Editor
Robert L. Wiser, Designer

Printed in Singapore

DISPLAY PHOTOGRAPHS

Endpapers: Room receipts from 1909 and 1910.
Page 1: A Brown Palace luggage tag from the 1950s.
Page 2: The sandstone facade with its frieze and
carvings.
Page 3: The hotel, dwarfed by Denver's modern sky-
scrapers.
Page 4: Tea in the Brown Palace Lounge sometime
between 1911 and 1920.
Page 5: The atrium lobby, where tea is still served.
Page 6: The Dutch Grill Room, opened in 1903 for
men only.
Page 7: The Brown Palace Club, the pride of
Denver's business community.
Pages 8–9: Early postcard views of the arch at
Union Station, the Brown Palace at night, and the
hotel's atrium lobby.
Pages 10–11: Onyx walls, a hallmark of Brown
Palace elegance.
Pages 16–17: An 1889 perspective map of Denver
showing the triangular plats abutting Broadway.
Pages 36–37: The hotel's Broadway facade, with
"The H. C. Brown Hotel" carved in sandstone on
the tower.
Pages 56–57: The Onyx Room, named for its
original onyx wainscoting.
Pages 80–81: The Grand Ballroom, which opened in
1959 and was renovated in 2002.
Page 104: A Brown Palace doorman's hat.

ILLUSTRATION CREDITS

All illustrations courtesy of the Brown Palace Hotel
except for the following:
Associated Press: 75
Berkeley Studios: 69 bottom right
Bradford-Robinson Printing Company, Denver: 54
bottom
Denver Public Library, Western History
Department, 2, 6, 13, 18–19, 19, 21 top, 22 bottom
left, 22 bottom middle, 22 bottom right, 23, 24,
25 bottom, 29 bottom left, 36–37, 39 top left, 40
top right, 44, 45 bottom left and right, 48, 49
both, 51 bottom, 54 top, 58 top left and right, 59,
61, 62, 63, 64 right, 69 top left, 77 all
Colorado Historical Society: 20, 39 top right, 40 top
left, 60 left
Fred G. Cook: 69 top right
Vicki Dochterman-Rienks: 73 inset
M & L Edwards: 74
Henry Fechtman: 7, 12, 14 both, 29, 30, 31 bottom,
32 center and bottom, 56–57, 58 bottom, 66 top,
80–81, 86, 89 bottom, 96, 98 all, 99, 100
Fisher and Fisher Architects, Denver: 52
James Havey: 95
E. C. Kropp Company, Milwaukee: 29 bottom right
Lainson Studio, Denver: 55 bottom right, 66 bottom
right, 94 bottom
Lake County (Illinois) Discovery Museum, Curt
Teich Postcard Archives: 8 both, 9, 21 bottom
Larry Laszlo: 69 bottom left
Leib Image Archives, York, Pa.: 15
Library of Congress: jacket, 16–17, 22 top, 26–27
bottom
Mile High Photo Company, Denver: 65 top, 67, 82,
87 right, 90 bottom left
Calvin H. Morse Family: 4, 38, 40 bottom, 41, 42,
43, 46 all, 47 all, 78, 92 right
Bill Peery: 70 all, 71 all, 72–73
Lynn Radeka: 91, 97
Margie Setvin Redlick: 51 top, 84 top
Robert Reck: 5, 10–11, 93, 101, 102, 103
Rocky Mountain Photo Company: 35 bottom right
Robert W. Schott, Denver: 53 left top, 53 left
middle, 79 bottom left
Scientific American: 25 top
Frank S. Thayer, Denver: 29 top left
Wonderworks, 31 top

CONTENTS

FOREWORD

Thank you for purchasing this history of the Brown Palace. Those of us at Quorum Hotels and Resorts are pleased to have been the custodian of the Brown Palace Hotel since 1987. We have seen some challenging times since our involvement, but we have always held the traditions and best interests of the Brown Palace Hotel as our primary goal.

The citizens of Denver have remained loyal and dedicated to the Brown Palace Hotel through good times and bad. We have been fortunate to have had the financial resources and structure to allow us to protect the Brown Palace's unique vintage conditions and to modernize where the guest will accept nothing less than current technology. There is something special about enjoying a Victorian-designed guest room while using the high-speed Internet.

The real strengths of the Brown Palace Hotel are not just its atrium lobby and fine restaurants. The hallmark of the Brown Palace has always been service, and service depends on dedicated employees. Those of us at Quorum Hotels and Resorts are very proud of the service our excellent staff provides around the clock. These staff members are carrying on the proud traditions that have allowed the Brown Palace Hotel to operate at a luxury level continuously since August 12, 1892. Few hotels in the United States can make this claim, and even fewer can live up to it.

We hope you enjoy the Brown Palace and encourage your family, friends, and associates to always think of the Brown Palace when they visit Denver. Enjoy!

W. Anthony Farris, Chairman
Quorum Hotels & Resorts

During the hotel's early days, the main entrance was on Broadway, at the base of the central tower. An ornately carved sandstone crest (above), still visible to the left of the Broadway arch, displays the initials of the hotel's founder, Henry C. Brown. An etching from 1892 (opposite), the year the Brown Palace opened, shows guests arriving by coach.

The Brown Palace captures the imagination as few old buildings can, evoking a time and a place missing from standard Old West histories. Although the hotel's elegant halls and lobby atrium have hosted gunfights and cattle rustlers, gamblers and soiled doves, today the landmark conjures up not cowboys and mountain men but the movers and shakers who built a city from its bar stools. The sweeping curve of the grand staircase recalls the grace of ladies who wove an elegant society in its tea rooms. And the intricate patterns of the atrium banisters trace the web of tragic romances and small dramas of the thousands of lives that passed through its onyx halls.

There is some debate as to whether Henry Cordes Brown or William H. Bush conceived the idea to build a grand hotel on the triangular patch at Seventeenth Street, Broadway, and Tremont Place. With money raised in England, Bush and his English friend James Duff excavated the foundation in 1888 but ran out of capital before construction could begin. After a time they persuaded Brown, a local developer from whom they had received a provisional contract for the land, to build the hotel. On Brown's behalf, Bush agreed to manage this marvel of construction—the hotel that opened on August 12, 1892, as the H. C. Brown Palace. Without Brown, Denver might eventually have had a hotel as grand as his Palace, but he was the man who took the gamble and got it completed before the Silver Panic of 1893, which drastically changed Colorado's financial picture for a long time.

The Brown Palace, as one might expect, has hosted many colorful and famous guests over time, from that other Brown (the "unsinkable" one) to presidents and royalty and rock stars. Even before the hotel celebrated its first hundred years, it received two singular honors: inclusion in the National Register of Historic Places in April 1970 and recognition as a Denver landmark in October 1989. On October 2 of that year, the hotel accepted a plaque from Mayor Federico Peña, after which honored guests from the city, Historic Denver, Inc., the Colorado State Historical Society, the National Trust for Historic Preservation, and employees with more than thirty years of service were entertained at lunch.

If shadowy figures still frequent the Brown Palace, certainly the spirit of Henry Brown must return to the great hotel that bears his name, if only to look on his own likeness carved beside the old Broadway entrance.

Although the Brown Palace's original ogee-arched entrance on Broadway is no longer in use, the stone carvings are intact (above left). Among them is a profile carving of the hotel's founder,

Henry C. Brown (above right). Geddis and Seerie, contractors for the hotel, were so meticulous that they imported fine sea sand for the mortar to ensure uniformly thin joints between the stones.

The hotel's Seventeenth Street entrance (opposite) was originally guarded by large sandstone carvings of griffins, as shown in this 1930s view. The sculptures were removed sometime later.

A Palace in the Rockies

In 1873 Henry C. Brown built for himself a grand house in the center of the block bounded by Seventeenth and Eighteenth Avenues and between Broadway and Lincoln. This gabled barn, which he had built at the same time, stood beside the Broadway Theater. Later used as a residence, it was torn down in the 1920s and replaced by a filling station.

THE UNFLAPPABLE
HENRY BROWN

In 1860, two years after the Denver City Town Company was organized in November 1858 by William H. Larimer Jr., Henry Cordes Brown (1820–1906) came to town, driving an ox cart that carried all his worldly goods, his wife, and his child. It was one of many journeys Brown had made since he had left Ohio as an orphan. In 1852 he had traveled to California with an ox team, walking, it was said, most of the way. He spent some time in San Francisco and then went to Puget Sound in Washington, where he worked in lumbering for almost a year. Back in San Francisco, he reportedly made a fortune as a builder. He then took passage to South America and spent time in Peru, although none of the records of his life recounted what he did there.

Brown found his way to Decatur, Nebraska, where he built a hotel and, when the new town failed to prosper, lost his fortune. He spent one year in St. Louis before heading for Denver, the jumping-off place for the mining boom that stimulated the nation's gold and silver fever. Other speculators were rushing to the hills in search of their fortunes. Brown, perhaps weary of traveling, decided to stay at the confluence of the South Platte River and Cherry Creek to build the stores and houses where prospectors would return to find supplies and settle down with their newfound wealth.

In 1864 he filed a preemption claim on a quarter section of land in the hills far east of the settlement of Denver. Here he put up a small frame house and, as required by law, bought the 160 acres of land for $200 and obtained title on December 1, 1865. Brown's homesteading secured his reputation as a colorful figure: the

Denver City Town Company claimed Brown's land and sent R. E. Whitsitt to order the apparent claim jumper off the land. Hatchet in hand, Brown made it clear that he had no intention of getting out.

Brown was later offered $500 for the entire tract but turned it down. The man who had made the offer reportedly told people he was glad he got out of the deal, because "that sand hill" was not worth $500 and never would be. In time, of course, it became Denver's exclusive Capitol Hill and made Brown a very rich man.

As a newcomer to the Rockies, Henry C. Brown relied on his carpentry skills to make a living. But he was also a savvy businessman, and his many enterprises, including the Brown Palace Hotel, made him a wealthy man. Brown was married three times and had five children.

Henry Brown contributed much more than a fine hostelry to his adopted city. His first building in Denver was a carpentry shop, which the congregation of the future Trinity Methodist Church began renting in February 1863 for $21 a month. The carpentry shop washed away in the flood of 1864, but the congregation's 1888 replacement would become a neighbor of his future hotel. In 1872, when the *Denver Daily* was unable to pay a debt owed to Brown, the paper passed into his hands. He moved it into a building he owned, renamed it the *Denver Tribune,* and ran it until 1875. On the first day of 1873 Brown and C. D. Gurley opened the Bank of Denver in a corner of Brown's Tribune Building. Although Brown was president of the bank, he sold his interest at the end of the year. When the chamber of commerce created the city's first library in 1885, Brown contributed the first $1,000.

By 1886 Brown's affairs permeated Denver's booming business life. He was on the board of directors of the Denver Tramway Company, was a charter member of the Board of Trade, and helped ensure that the Denver Pacific, which ran between Denver and Cheyenne, Wyoming, was the first railroad into the city.

When the territorial legislature in 1867 settled on Denver rather than Golden as the territorial capital, Brown "clinched the proposition by stepping forward with a donation of 10 acres of land for a capitol site," according to Jerome Smiley's *History of Denver* (1901). The territorial government, however, never got around to erecting a building on the site. When the territory was dissolved in 1876 and the state of Colorado established, Brown maintained that the land should revert to him. In 1884 he sued, seeking to regain the property, but lost. So the capitol building was built on land he donated, albeit a bit unwillingly, to the new state.

One year after the Brown Palace opened, the Silver Panic of 1893 wiped out many Colorado fortunes and left Brown, at the age of seventy-three, no longer a rich man. Yet the next year he married a nineteen-year-old grocery store cashier. Divorce ended the marriage about six years later, and although the young woman remarried soon thereafter, the newspapers reported that Brown was most gracious, calling on the newlyweds and wishing them happiness. His ex-wife returned many of the gifts he had given her, save for one necklace of which she was extremely fond.

Henry Cordes Brown died in San Diego in 1906 at the age of eighty-five. Permission was given by the governor for his body to lie in state in the Colorado capitol, built on the land Brown had donated. He is buried in Denver's Fairmount Cemetery, where he and the architect of the Brown Palace both found lasting peace.

Designed in the Beaux-Arts style, the Colorado State Capitol (above) was a source of pride to the state's citizens. Construction, which began in 1890, was finally completed in 1908. Frank E. Edbrooke, architect of the Brown Palace, oversaw the final phases of construction.

The capitol (left) sits on ten acres of land donated by Brown, whose portrait hangs in the building's main entrance.

Denver's Capitol Hill neighborhoods reflect Brown's insistence on platting his land on a north-south, east-west grid, in contrast with the Denver City Town Company's angled plats. Sherman Street (opposite) was one of many streets Brown named for Civil War heroes.

Through a variety of buildings, Frank E. Edbrooke, one of Denver's preeminent architects, left his imprint on the city's cultural, intellectual, and commercial life. The Tabor Grand Opera House (1879) (top), located at the corner of Sixteenth and Curtis Streets, provided the main stage for Denver culture for

three-quarters of a century. For Loretto Heights College, Edbrooke designed Old Main (1891) (above left), the first building on campus. One of his commercial buildings was the Cooper Building (1892) (above middle), built at the corner of Seventeenth and Curtis Streets. Edbrooke's own home (above right), at

931 East Seventeenth Avenue, was in the Queen Anne style, one of the fashionable residential styles of the day. For the Colorado State Museum (1913) (opposite), at Fourteenth Avenue and Sherman Street, he turned to the Beaux-Arts style to produce a beautiful, classically inspired civic structure that still stands.

Frank E. Edbrooke (1840–1921), a Civil War veteran, came to Denver from Chicago in 1879 with his architect brother, Willoughby J. Edbrooke (1843–96). Willoughby had been enticed west by Leadville's silver king, Horace A. W. Tabor, who wanted to shake things up architecturally in Denver. The brothers obliged with the polychrome Tabor Grand Opera House (1879; demolished 1964) and the Tabor Block (1880; demolished 1972). Although Willoughby, whose son Harry eventually joined the family profession, moved on to design federal buildings across the country, Frank stayed in Denver, becoming one of the city's most esteemed architects.

With the Edbrookes came the eclectic Victorian architectural styles that were changing the face of cities east of the new capital. For the entrepreneur Jerome B. Wheeler, the brothers produced in Aspen the Wheeler Opera House (1889), whose rough-faced Romanesque Revival walls hid a glittering theater inside. When the original architect of the state capitol was dismissed in 1889, Frank Edbrooke stepped in to complete the building, changing the dome's copper skin to gold and substituting elaborate capitals on the portico's columns. More work soon came his way: in 1890 he designed the Masonic Temple, the Broadway Theater, and the Oxford Hotel on Seventeenth Street, built around what is thought to be the city's first steel-skeleton frame.

In 1889 or 1890 Henry Brown made a point of asking this eminent architect to design his own hotel at the other end of Seventeenth Street. To fit the obtuse angle that resulted from the platting of Brown's 160-acre homestead, known as Brown's Addition after it was annexed by the city of Denver, Edbrooke chose the style in which he had become so accomplished—the Richardsonian Romanesque—wrapping his three-sided masterpiece around a dramatic skylighted atrium. At nine stories, it was a marvel: Denver's tallest building.

Edbrooke went on to create many more local landmarks, including the Central Presbyterian Church (1878); The Navarre (1880), now a private office building; Old Main (1891) for Loretto Heights College; the Denver Dry Goods Company Building (1894); the old Spratlen-Anderson Warehouse (1906), now called Edbrooke Lofts; and the Colorado State Museum (1913). His own home on Seventeenth Avenue, designed in 1893, is a delightful Queen Anne residence of brick and stone; it stands next door to another design of his, now converted into a bed-and-breakfast. Edbrooke also designed a mausoleum for himself at Fairmount Cemetery. It was his last work, and he was buried there after his death on May 3, 1921.

23

For Henry Brown's hotel on an awkward triangular site, Frank Edbrooke envisioned an Italian Renaissance–style building with romanesque arcaded windows, multiple cornices, and horizontal banding to counteract the thrilling nine-story height. Inspiration came from his hometown of Chicago, then in the midst of a building boom following the Great Fire of 1871, in particular the Marshall Field Wholesale Store (1885), designed by Henry Hobson Richardson, and the world-renowned Auditorium Building (1887), designed by Louis Sullivan.

Edbrooke chose a sturdy base of red Pikes Peak granite that balanced walls of red Arizona sandstone. Repeating the Renaissance arch motif, unusual ogee arches embellish the three original entrances, and giant arches rise from the fourth through the seventh floors. James Whitehouse (1842–1904), an artist newly arrived in Denver, was commissioned to carve twenty-six stone medallions depicting native Rocky Mountain animals such as big horn sheep, elk, and bison, each set between the seventh-floor windows. Other stone trim included a bas-relief bust of Brown himself and a cornice announcing "The H. C. Brown Hotel." Within twenty years the hotel's exterior was in need of cleaning and repair. In about 1910 all the sandstone and granite surfaces were sandblasted, resulting in the inadvertent destruction of much of the stone ornamentation.

The hotel's triangular design guaranteed that every guest room faced a street. Colorado had "sunshine on tap" at the Brown Palace, wrote an English visitor, because guests were asked when they registered whether they preferred the morning or the afternoon sun and were roomed accordingly. There were no buildings nearby to block the sun or the view. Only the tower of Trinity Methodist Church (1888) and the Metropole Hotel (1890; demolished), later the Plaza Cosmopolitan, shared Broadway with the new hotel.

Blueprints for the Brown Palace required nearly two tons of paper, reported the journal *Scientific American* in its May 21, 1892, issue. The article went on to describe the unique design features of the atrium lobby. Measuring 56 feet square, the open interior court was "covered with a flat ceiling of stained glass and plated iron ribs suspended at the ninth floor." The ceiling was created by the Watkins Glass Company, a local company founded in 1868 and still in operation today. A skylight supported by steel trusses was installed above the glass to protect the ceiling from the elements. In 1936, when the Brown Palace was renovated, a proposal was made to enclose the center court at the third level. Fortunately, the proposal was never enacted, and the stunning eight-story atrium remains. The stained glass ceiling is never artificially illuminated, allowing Colorado's sunshine to fill the hotel's lobby with natural light every day.

24

Henry Brown's cow pasture (opposite)—
a triangular plot of land bounded
by Broadway, Seventeenth Street, and
Tremont Place—became the site of the
Brown Palace.

The Brown Palace was considered
a marvel of construction in its day.
The May 21, 1892, issue of *Scientific
American* featured on its cover this illustration of the hotel's interior construction (above). It shows the great steel
beams in place; to the side are stacks of
hollow blocks of porous terra cotta for
use in the floors and walls.

With the Brown Palace's grand opening
approaching, construction workers
took a break from laying tile inside to
pose with their dog at the Broadway
entrance (right).

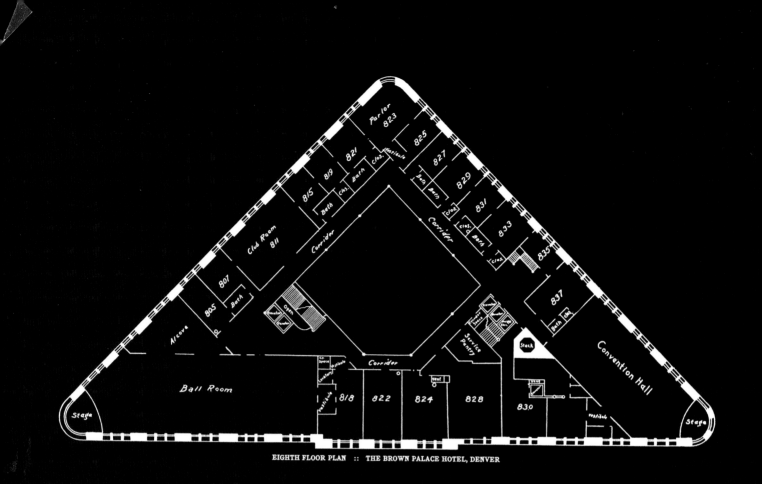

EIGHTH FLOOR PLAN :: THE BROWN PALACE HOTEL, DENVER

This plan of the Brown Palace's eighth floor (opposite) shows the original location of the hotel's ballroom, where an elaborate banquet was held on opening night, August 12, 1892.

Carriages deposit guests at the Brown Palace in an 1892 sketch (right). During the next century open carriages and elegant broughams gave way first to automobiles and then to touring bus coaches and airport shuttles.

Looking west to the front range of the Rocky Mountains, this 1898 panoramic view of Denver (below) shows the buildings arrayed along Broadway, including the Brown Palace (right in photograph) and Frank Edbrooke's Majestic Building (1894), one block to the south. Across Sixteenth Street and one block to the west of Broadway is the domed Arapahoe County Courthouse. Visible at the far right is the steeple of Trinity Methodist Church, constructed in 1888.

A FIREPROOF WONDER

The Brown Palace was declared absolutely fireproof—one of the first such buildings in the country. No wood was used. Instead, the hotel was framed with wrought-iron and steel columns. All floors and partition walls were built of hollow blocks of porous terra cotta and surfaced with fireproof cement. Floor blocks were shaped to surround the beams and columns, thus protecting the iron from fire. Tests proved that the terra cotta could withstand 1,800-degree heat. When an elderly woman guest was told about the fireproofing, she was reported to have said, "Wal, I dunno as I sh'd mind findin' myself in Hades if I could be sent down shet up in one of these bedrooms, like a turtle in his shell."

Fifteen main ventilation shafts ran from the basement to the roof, housing hot and cold water pipes, tank supplies, toilet flushes, vents, soil pipes, and circulation pipes with electric fans on top to draw the air from all the bedrooms and bathrooms through open registers in the bathroom walls. "If the stealthy microbe gains admission, instead of lurking in some dark corner until he can pounce upon his prey," asserted a gift booklet prepared for the hotel's first guests, "he finds himself in a sort of maelstrom of fresh air, and is rapidly whirled onward and upwards till he presumably congeals in the frigid upper regions." The shafts were so large that workmen could crawl inside for inspection and repairs.

Other unique interior elements included steam heat, an engine room that "might well be the den of Edison himself," the largest private electric plant in Colorado, an ice machine capable of making five tons of ice a day, six Hale hydraulic elevators, and two artesian wells 750 feet deep. The hotel also housed its own laundry and claimed that the refuse burner could, if a guest should make such a gruesome request, serve as a crematory. It is nowhere recorded that a guest ever did so request.

Eleven graceful arches, embellished with a repeating egg-and-dart pattern, frame the atrium on the second floor of the Brown Palace (opposite).

The hotel's three entrances allowed access to Denver's financial, shopping, business, and theater districts. This is the Seventeenth Street entrance (left).

The "Onyx Lobby," its solid onyx pillars still in place, remains relatively unchanged. Guests are welcomed at the same front desk (bottom left). A 1920s postcard (bottom right) shows the addition of oriental carpets, plush furniture, and potted plants.

Art objects from the Napoleonic era were collected to create an authentic atmosphere for the Palace Arms restaurant. An elegant army helmet (opposite) is displayed on each side of the entry.

Unveiled on New Year's Eve 1999, this specially commissioned clock (left) was sculpted by the noted artist Robert Shure. As the griffins stood their watchful guard, the clock's chimes rang in the year 2000 and proclaimed the timepiece's permanent home above the front desk.

The lobby walls (below) beckoned to the soldiers of the U.S. Army's Tenth Mountain Division, who tried rappelling from the balconies while stationed here during World War II.

Luminous paintings and detailed ironwork (top left) provide the finishing touches for the Brown Palace's magnificent atrium lobby.

An ornate silver drinking fountain in the lobby (top center), one of a pair, offers visitors a chance to sample water from the hotel's artesian wells.

Electric wall sconces have ornamented the lobby's onyx columns since opening day (top right).

Two large lobby murals painted in 1937 by Allen True, a local artist, depict the evolution of travel in the West from stagecoach to airplane (left middle and bottom). Speculation has it that the man in the trench coat is the late Howard Hughes and the woman stepping off the plane is the late great golfer Babe Deidrickson Zaharias. While the resemblances are striking, no one is sure if this was True's intent.

Surrounding the atrium on each floor are railings of ironwork panels (opposite) made by the Chicago Ornamental Ironworks Company. Two of the copper-finished panels were installed upside down.

It took four years and $1.6 million to turn Frank Edbrooke's design into reality and another $400,000 to furnish the hotel with the finest fittings: Axminster, Wilton, and Brussels carpets; Irish Point, Cluny, and Brussels net curtains; Irish linen; Haviland, Limoges, and Royal Doulton china; and Reed and Barton silver. The furniture was solid white mahogany, antique oak, and cherry. Chairs and sofas were covered in silk.

The four hundred guest rooms were evenly divided by price: one hundred at $3 a night, one hundred at $4 a night, one hundred at $4.50 a night, and, the top of the line, one hundred at $5 a night. Not only was there a mammoth fireplace in the lobby (now the entrance to a gift shop), but each guest room also boasted its own fireplace. Guests could simply call the desk to have a bellboy bring up kindling and coal.

A 300-mile panorama of Rocky Mountain grandeur awaited the two hundred and fifty guests who could be seated in the eighth-floor dining room. The room was two stories high, with panels of stained glass in fruit designs above each window and onyx wainscoting five feet high. On the same floor was a banquet hall–ballroom, also two stories high, and six private dining rooms, including a "ladies' ordinary" and a club room for gentlemen. The kitchen too was on the top floor, "thus securing perfect ventilation, and banishing all malodorous ghosts of dead and gone dinners from every part of the house," enthusiastically declared the hotel's first promotional publication.

Shortly after the construction contract for the hotel was signed, an onyx mine was discovered in Torreon, Mexico, by the Denver Onyx and Marble Manufacturing Company, so onyx was used for the hotel's interior paneling. When completed, 12,400 superficial feet of the stone, more than previously used in a single building, had been incorporated into the Brown Palace lobby, the Grand Salon, and the eighth-floor ballroom. Copper-finished railings on each floor gave "the effect of antique solid copper" to the iron-and-steel panels (although the copper eventually lost its burnished look).

"Such perfect harmony of softly blending colors is seen nowhere else, save perhaps in Italian sunset skies," rhapsodized the guest booklet. "One fancies the gnomes who for centuries so jealously guarded the mine, stealing from countless beds of tropical flowers their choicest tints and embalming them in their exquisite stone."

Although the finishing work was not quite complete, the hotel hosted its first guests, the Twenty-fifth Triennial Conclave of Knights Templar, on August 12, 1892. Many guests had to sleep on cots in the halls, but there was nothing improvised about the formal banquet. The seven-course dinner cost $10 a plate and included a beverage list showing 227 wines, mineral waters, and champagnes.

The Brown Palace bridal suites, an example of which was depicted in an early hotel brochure (left), were appointed with sumptuous carpeting, solid brass bedsteads, and floral accents on the drapes, bed canopy, and silk finishing.

On the hotel's opening day a formal banquet for the Twenty-fifth Triennial Conclave of Knights Templar was held in the ballroom (opposite top). Several hundred people attended the event. The menu (opposite bottom left) listed mountain trout and golden plover as well as Maryland terrapin. In addition to magnificent balls of up to three hundred couples, the ballroom could also accommodate concerts and meetings (opposite bottom right).

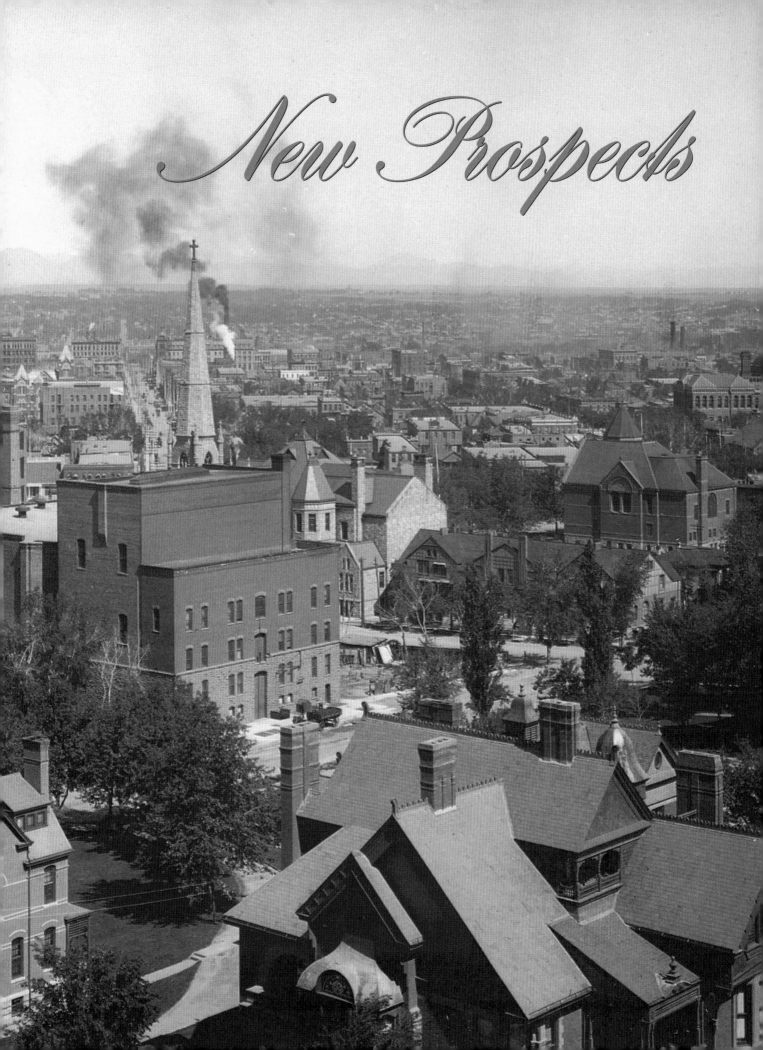

New Prospects

Henry Brown chose William H. Bush and N. Maxcy Tabor to jointly manage his new hotel. Bush had been involved with the hotel from the beginning, having helped finance the excavation. An Ohio native like Brown, he had spent time in Leadville with Horace Tabor, helping build and then managing Tabor's Clarendon Hotel. He also managed Tabor's Windsor Hotel in Denver and the Teller House in Central City.

Maxcy Tabor was the son of Augusta and Horace Tabor. He too had learned the hotel business at his father's Clarendon and Windsor Hotels and had inherited Tabor's taste for luxury. He was responsible for spending the $400,000 that it cost to furnish the hotel.

Bush owned the 480-acre Windsor Farms a few miles outside Denver. The farm's three hundred cows supplied all the fresh milk, cream, and butter for the Brown Palace and Bush's own Metropole Hotel. The entire production of its vegetable gardens and orchards went to the Brown and the Metropole, and guests of each could be driven to the farm for outings.

Interested in the theater, Bush built the Broadway Theater, which opened on August 28, 1890, across the street from the site of the Brown Palace and next door to the Metropole. He was a partner of Peter McCourt (the

brother of Horace Tabor's second wife, Baby Doe) in the Colorado Amusement Company, which managed the Tabor Grand Opera House and the Broadway Theater. When Horace Tabor's sagging fortunes forced the sale of the Opera House in 1896, McCourt was ousted as manager, and Bush made him manager of the Broadway.

Bush died in 1898—in debt and intestate, like so many of his contemporaries. Three years later his daughter, Marie Antoinette Singers-Bigger, filed suit against the McCourts. Arguing that McCourt had acquired his money as a result of her father's generosity, she sought a share of the Colorado Amusement Company's profits. In 1907 she was awarded $47,100, and the papers reported that "an hour after the money was paid, exchange on the Bank of England was in the mails on its way to London," where she was living, the wife of a minor member of the peerage.

Maxcy Tabor served as treasurer of his father's Opera House, engaged in mining in Leadville, and became president of the Green River Petroleum Company, which had its offices in the Majestic Building (1894), also designed by Edbrooke. Tabor and the Bush heirs remained principal stockholders in the Brown Hotel Company. Tabor died in 1929 at the age of seventy, having spent many years trying to gain control of the Brown Palace.

The furnishings for the Brown Palace—including walnut furniture and silk mohair upholstery for the guest rooms (opposite)—were supplied by the Robert Mitchell Furniture Company of Cincinnati.

Denver's hotel district (right) offered many choices for visitors to the Queen City of the Plains, but only the Brown Palace has operated continuously for more than a century. The Brown Palace's first managers, William Bush and Maxcy Tabor, had previously worked at the Windsor Hotel (above left), at Eighteenth and Larimer Streets, which had opened in 1880. Bush and Otto Kappler also managed the Hotel Metropole (1890) (above right), directly across Broadway from the Brown Palace.

1239-HOTEL DISTRICT on BROADWAY, DENVER, COLO.

When they opened the Brown Palace in 1892, William Bush (far left) and Maxcy Tabor (left) were veteran hoteliers. The two men oversaw every detail of the hotel's daily operations.

Brown Palace guests today still sign in at the original front desk, shown about 1915 (below).

The Main Dining Room (opposite top and bottom), located in the space now occupied by Ellyngton's, was decorated in the French Renaissance manner. Gold-lacquered chairs upholstered in soft blue panne velvet, windows swathed in rich draperies and curtains, ornate ceilings—all created a beautiful room and a memorable dining experience.

To meet pressing debts, Henry Brown took out loans on the Brown Palace Hotel totaling $800,000. He was so heavily mortgaged that by 1898 foreclosure of the Brown Palace was imminent, with Maxcy Tabor trying to persuade the U.S. Mortgage Company to foreclose on the loans. Fearing that Tabor might then gain control of the hotel, Brown's son James approached W. S. Stratton, a Cripple Creek millionaire.

Winfield Scott Stratton (1848–1902) was one of the most interesting figures to play a role in the Brown Palace story. In many ways he took after his famous namesake, the Mexican War hero General Winfield Scott, and was even nicknamed "Little Fuss and Feathers" (the general was called "Fuss and Feathers"). Stratton had been apprenticed to a carpenter yet always dreamed of the West and of finding gold out there some day. He saved up $300 and set out for Pikes Peak, arriving in Colorado Springs in 1872.

Stratton found immediate employment with a friend, James D. Raymond, another "hustler," according to Frank Waters, Stratton's biographer, in *Midas of the Rockies* (1937). Two years later the young man from Indiana went into a partnership as a carpenter and contractor-builder, but the old dream of finding gold still drove him, and he sold the business in 1874 to go prospecting. Instead of finding gold, he lost his money, and he turned back to carpentry.

Although Stratton had been a fairly popular young bachelor around Colorado Springs, his first failure at mining and an unhappy marriage in 1876, which ended in divorce three years later, changed him completely. He became something of a recluse, "a carpenter without a job and a prospector who had never made a strike," according to Waters.

When silver was discovered in Leadville, Stratton went there. He watched other men, among them Horace Tabor, strike it rich, but his own efforts failed. While Stratton was looking for his big strike, a man named Tom Walsh made a mining fortune in Leadville. Several years later Walsh's wealth enabled his daughter Evalyn to keep a suite at the Brown Palace.

For seventeen years Stratton trudged the mountains, looking for the lucky strike that would make him as rich as Tabor and Walsh. Finally he went back to school to study metallurgy at the Colorado School of Mines in Golden, and what he learned there led to his discovery of the Independence Mine in Cripple Creek on July 4, 1891, one of the state's most lucrative mines. With his first earnings from the mine, which in the end produced more than $28 million worth of gold, he hunted up every stockholder in his previous failed mining ventures and repaid all their losses.

Now that he was rich, "Little London," as Colorado Springs became known, expected Stratton to build a fine house and make a big social splash. Instead, he bought a modest home, one that he had built during his early contracting days, and installed his widowed sister as his housekeeper. Instead of buying himself a fine carriage, he paid an old cab driver $300 to sleep in the cab outside his office and to take him wherever he wanted to go. His only extravagance was to have an old German shoemaker, Bob Schwarz, make him a pair of fine boots. He was so pleased that he made Schwarz general manager of all his mining properties.

Although he never joined a church and was often at odds with the clergy, Stratton contributed to the building of many churches in Colorado Springs. Every Christmas he sent coal to every poor family in the neighboring mining town of Victor, and he made generous gifts to the Salvation Army. In spite of his generosity, however, the eccentric Stratton was never fully accepted.

43

By 1915 the hotel had installed an electrically lighted vertical sign at the Seventeenth Street and Tremont Place corner (opposite). Although several stories high, it read simply "Brown."

The rooms reflected simple elegance (right). The hotel's linens, bedding, and carpets were procured from Daniels and Fisher Company of Denver at a cost of $21,680.

In 1898, when Horace Tabor was down on his luck, W. S. Stratton, whose nickname was "Midas of the Rockies," gave the old "Silver King" $15,000. Tabor insisted on securing the deal with a note and a deed to a mine in Arizona. Stratton did not bother to record the deed, and a few months before Tabor died in poverty in 1899, Stratton returned it. Apparently it did not do Tabor and his second wife, Baby Doe, any good. Found among their effects was the deed with the scrawled note: "We thought that Mr. Stratton had recorded this deed, it would have saved it for us; too bad." Because it had remained in Tabor's name, the banks had foreclosed on the mine along with all the Tabors' other property.

In April 1900 for $800,000 Stratton acquired the mortgage of the Brown Palace Hotel, the principal item in the estate of Jane C. Brown (Henry's second wife, who died in 1893), but did not take title to the property, an attempt to give the family a chance to sell the hotel without losing it to foreclosure. The new owner assured Henry Brown that he could live out his final years in the hotel that bore his name—the kind of gesture for which Stratton was famous.

In 1901 Stratton took possession of the Brown Palace; title was taken by his real estate holding company, and all claims against the Brown estate were settled, although the Brown family retained the right to repurchase the hotel. Over the next five years numerous attempts were made by Maxcy Tabor and others to purchase the hotel,

since the Browns were unable to do so. Stratton died in 1902, leaving the hotel with an unpaid mortgage of $650,000. In 1904 the courts declared that the Brown Palace must be sold to satisfy its mortgage claims. Foreclosure was imminent.

In 1908 the Stratton estate paid the Brown heirs for the release from their right to purchase the Brown Palace and took possession of the hotel. Two years later the Stratton estate transferred the title to the Brown Palace, now valued at $1.5 million, to the Myron Stratton Home Corporation, a home for the indigent aged founded by Stratton and named for his father. Built after Stratton's death, the home fulfilled his desire to aid the elderly so that they would not have to work hard or to go without good food and comfortable clothing.

Henry Brown's son, James Henry Brown, also found himself involved in some complex financial dealings as a result of Stratton's generosity. James, the baby who had come west in the ox cart with his parents, had long since established himself as well-respected lawyer in Denver and in 1885 became Denver's first elected city attorney. However, his greatest legal challenge was the tangled web of Brown Palace ownership. From his initial contact with Stratton in 1898 until final title transfer to the Myron Stratton Home Corporation in 1910, James Brown oversaw more than a decade of continuous litigation concerning the Brown Palace mortgage.

Denver sightseeing companies picked up tourists at the Brown Palace in vehicles similar to this one (above). The Seeing Denver Car Company even had a theme song with the lyrics "Now look up the street and a vision you'll meet, the Brown Palace stands right in view."

The lives and financial affairs of Horace Tabor (left), Leadville's "Silver King," and W. S. Stratton (right), known for his generosity, were intertwined with the history of the Brown Palace. When Tabor was down on his luck, Stratton stepped in to help.

Tabor's grand house (opposite) at 1260 Sherman Street, which he purchased in 1886 for $54,000, set the tone for his fashionable Capitol Hill neighborhood.

Putting a calm face on the hotel's ownership squabbles was Calvin H. Morse
(left in top left photograph), the Brown
Palace's general manager from 1910 to
1923. Before joining the Brown Palace
staff, Morse had managed the Oxford
Hotel (1891), located at 1600 Seventeenth Street and designed by Frank E.
Edbrooke. At the Brown Palace he
oversaw every facet of its operations—
from its 1910 remodelings to its hosting
of the Elks Convention of 1914 (opposite
top). Staff members (middle) were
proud to work for Morse, and
influential people called him a friend;
their kind words and mementos recall
an earlier time (bottom left and right).
A custodian of Brown Palace history,
Morse kept a personal scrapbook filled
with letters and photographs (top right
and opposite bottom) chronicling
Denver life in the early 1900s.

To C H Morse
Ah there!

Walter Gen Emerson
1915

In 1911, when President William Howard Taft entered the Brown Palace lobby (above) for the first time, he delayed his escort for five minutes to admire the atrium's commanding beauty.

Charles Boettcher I (opposite left)— a German immigrant who became a merchant, industrial promoter, and banker—was a Colorado success story. His prosperity enabled him to build a

grand house (opposite right) in 1890 on Capitol Hill at Twelfth and Grant Streets. Boettcher spent a mere $26,000 on its construction, a modest amount compared to what Horace Tabor spent for his house.

The hotel's next owners were Charles Boettcher and Horace W. Bennett, who bought the hotel in 1922 from the Myron Stratton Home Corporation. While W. S. Stratton was still a poor carpenter pounding nails in Leadville, Boettcher was a hardware merchant there with better luck: he reportedly sold a $20 cookstove to a prospector for shares in a mine that netted him $150,000. Bennett had tramped the hills of Cripple Creek, dealing in real estate.

Boettcher came to America from Germany in 1869, a seventeen-year-old secondary school graduate. He was soon at work with his brother Herman in Cheyenne, Wyoming, learning the hardware trade along with English and how to make money in business. Charles was left in charge of the store in 1871 but ended up in Fort Collins the next year. There he married Fannie Augusta Cowan in 1874 and soon after sold the business and moved to Boulder, where for the first time the name C. Boettcher and Company was displayed. Boulder had railroad service, so Charles began buying his stock in wholesale lots directly off the rails (he once had some two hundred stoves for sale), enabling him to undercut his competitors. A son, Claude Kedzie, was born in Boulder in 1875, and four years later the family moved to booming Leadville.

In Leadville, C. Boettcher and Company was located just across from the new Clarendon Hotel, managed by the same William H. Bush who was later to manage the Brown Palace. Boettcher began manufacturing blasting powder, which previously had been brought in from California or the East, often exploding en route. He soon invested in mining properties and established lasting busi-

ness relationships with men like Horace Tabor, John Campion, A. V. Hunter, and George W. Trimble—the carbonate kings who became leading Colorado bankers and whose families would become neighbors when the Boettchers moved to Denver's fashionable Capitol Hill in 1890.

The one-time hardware man—Boettcher's old store still stands on Pearl Street in Boulder—was involved in many enterprises, but about 1901, when he was nearly fifty and considered himself retired, he founded the two companies for which he is best remembered: the Great Western Sugar Company and the Ideal Cement Company (now Ideal Basic Industries), both of which operated throughout Colorado, Wyoming, and Nebraska. On a visit to his native Germany in 1900, Boettcher had studied the methods used in sugar beet production. To try growing the beets in Colorado, he and Fannie allegedly brought back some high-quality seed packed in her trunks—leaving some of her clothes behind. Then, while building the plants to process the sugar, he got interested in producing cement and started his own cement company, becoming one of the leading industrial tycoons in the Rocky Mountain region.

In 1920, five years after Charles and Fannie were separated, he moved into the Brown Palace. Two years later Boettcher and Bennett bought the hotel through their Fifteenth Street Investment Company, which they had formed in 1902. Boettcher maintained an apartment on the top floor of the Brown Palace until his death in 1948. His summer home on Lookout Mountain, built in 1916 of local granite, eventually became the Jefferson County Nature Center.

49

THE TORCH PASSES

When Horace W. Bennett had to liquidate some of his holdings during the Great Depression, Charles Boettcher and his son, Claude Kedzie, bought out Bennett's principal share of the Brown Palace in 1931. Charles thought it a poor investment, but C. K., as he became known, had faith that business conditions would improve. He guided the hotel through the Depression and World War II and was responsible for the creation of the Ship Tavern (1934), decoration of the Palace Arms (1950), and creation of the San Marco Room (1959), which opened after his death.

After the war outside developers—William Zeckendorf of New York City and the Murchisons of Dallas—began investing in Denver. For a time C. K. and Zeckendorf collaborated in plans to build a Hilton Hotel and a May D&F store on the old Courthouse Square. However, the two tycoons disagreed on the material to be used in construction. Zeckendorf wanted a steel skeleton, while C. K., understandably, insisted on concrete. Zeckendorf went on to build the Hilton alone, and C. K. began to plan a twenty-two-story hotel tower on Tremont Place across from the Brown Palace.

In 1937 the family had created the Boettcher Foundation, with Charles, C .K., and his son, Charles Boettcher II, as trustees, along with James Quigg Newton. Following the death of Charles II in 1963, the Brown Palace became a wholly owned subsidiary of the Foundation. Cris Dobbins, Charles Boettcher's closest aide, and Warren E. Willard, another associate, were faithful custodians of the ideals established for the hotel by C. K. Boettcher. They died within weeks of each other in 1979.

For a half century the Boettcher name was associated with the Brown Palace. In 1980 the hotel was sold to Associated Inns and Restaurants Company of America, and then in 1983 it was purchased by Integrated Resources. Beginning in 1987 it was managed by Quorum Hotels and Resorts of Dallas, known as Rank Hotels of North America. Today the hotel is owned by the Brown Palace Hotel Associates Limited Partnership and is managed by Quorum Hotels and Resorts. Although the hotel's tower, built in 1959, has been known by other names—Brown Palace West, Denver Inn, and Comfort Inn Downtown Denver—it is still owned and operated by the same companies. The Brown Palace is a charter member of Historic Hotels of America, sponsored by the National Trust for Historic Preservation.

The silk-draped Casanova Room (above) was the setting for a festive Christmas banquet given by Horace W. Bennett.

By the time Bennett and Charles Boettcher purchased the hotel in 1922, glass partitions had been added in the lobby and a commanding elk had taken up residence on the fireplace mantel (right).

Three generations—Charles Boettcher I, C. K. Boettcher, and Charles Boettcher II (opposite top, middle, and bottom)— guided the Brown Palace through the Great Depression, World War II, and numerous changes in the hospitality industry.

Each change in ownership of the Brown Palace brought plans for remodeling or talk of additions to the original structure. As early as 1902, Maxcy Tabor and D. H. Moffat proposed adding two stories to the original nine. In 1909, under Stratton's ownership, plans for adding three stories were drawn up but then abandoned.

In 1929, during the Bennett years, plans were drawn to make the hotel twenty-six stories tall, but the stock market plunge that October threw the country into the Great Depression. By the time the economy had recovered, the country was at war and the materials for such a structure, not to mention the labor, were no longer available.

Finally in 1957 C. K. Boettcher signed his approval for plans to build a twenty-two-story tower across Tremont Place and to remodel the original hotel building. On a day just short of his eighty-second birthday he held meetings with his staff regarding the new tower; a few hours later his heart failed him. A year after his death, Boettcher's family donated his 1908 Denver mansion for use as the Colorado governor's residence.

Despite Boettcher's death, plans for the tower proceeded. The new tower was designed by the architecture firm of William B. Tabler of New York City, which had designed hotels worldwide, including the International Hotel at Idlewild Airport in New York, the Dallas Statler-Hilton, and leading hotels in South America. The N. K. Petry Construction Company of Denver, long associated with remodeling projects at the Brown, was the building contractor, and Havens-Batchelder of Denver was in charge of the decorating.

Two years later, on April 25, 1959, the formal grand opening of the twenty-two-story Brown Palace West with its three hundred guest rooms was celebrated with an Old West costume ball, a benefit for Denver's Children's Hospital. Hollywood stars Lana Turner, Edgar

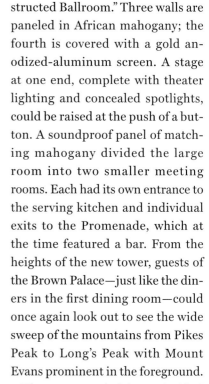

In 1929 Fisher and Fisher, a Denver architecture firm, presented this proposal for an addition that would make the Brown Palace twenty-six floors high, but it was never built.

Bergen, Linda Darnell, Rex Allen, and Hoagy Carmichael, together with Frankie Master's Orchestra and the vocalist Phyllis Myles, provided entertainment. On the menu were Pineapple Fraser, Trout Filet Almondine Gunnison, Beef Prime Rib Central City, Salad Grand Junction, and Baked Alaska Denver, ending with Champagne Centennial and Cafe Colorado.

Dinner was served in the tower's new ballroom, which the *Denver Post* described as "Denver's Finest Unobstructed Ballroom." Three walls are paneled in African mahogany; the fourth is covered with a gold anodized-aluminum screen. A stage at one end, complete with theater lighting and concealed spotlights, could be raised at the push of a button. A soundproof panel of matching mahogany divided the large room into two smaller meeting rooms. Each had its own entrance to the serving kitchen and individual exits to the Promenade, which at the time featured a bar. From the heights of the new tower, guests of the Brown Palace—just like the diners in the first dining room—could once again look out to see the wide sweep of the mountains from Pikes Peak to Long's Peak with Mount Evans prominent in the foreground.

The new tower's debut coincided with the city's "Rush to the Rockies" centennial celebration. During French Week, Alex Humbert, executive chef at Maxim's in Paris, came to handle the delights of the table. A near tragedy ensued when his specialty, the long-simmered Sauce Albert, was inadvertently disposed of by one of the kitchen staff. "Humbert trembled," wrote William J. Barker in the *Denver Post*'s "Wayward Reporter" column on September 9. "He thought most assuredly of killing himself. Next he thought of declaring war on the United States. . . ." Instead he raced to the kitchen, went back to work, and "laboring like mad, established a new world's record for creating Sauce Albert."

Once the pouring of twenty-two levels of cement was completed (top left), a rooftop "topping out" celebration was held in August 1958 (middle left). A brochure announced the grand opening on April 25, 1959 (bottom left). The tower's comfortable corner suites (top right) afforded views of the Rocky Mountains and downtown Denver. Visible through the open window is the Daniels and Fisher (D&F) tower (1912), located at Sixteenth and Arapahoe Streets, which once dominated the Denver skyline but is now dwarfed by taller buildings. In its first four decades the Grand Ballroom (above right) played host to more than fifteen thousand meetings and two thousand weddings and served more than eleven thousand meals, including those for more than one thousand charity events.

The Navarre (above) offered a plush and private place for gentlemen to entertain. Clandestine meetings were the order of the day.

The Sultan's Dream (left), by Virgilio Tojetti, was commissioned for the hotel's opening in 1892. The one decorative appointment continuously on public display, it presently hangs in the Churchill Bar.

To connect the historic 1892 hotel and the new tower, a bridge was built over Tremont Place and a service tunnel dug at basement level. An escalator now rises to the bridge from a new seating area just outside the Ship Tavern. A stained glass window layered with a wood carving of Colorado flora and fauna by the Littleton artist Edgar Britton (1901–82) originally looked out on Tremont Place from the base of the escalators, while a second Britton carving hung above the escalator, visible to those descending. (The window was replaced in the 1980s, and the art pieces were sold.)

Telephones and a pneumatic tube linked the tower's own registration desk with the main lobby across the street. Guests could check in or out using either lobby. An underground garage, served by an automatic car lift, provided parking for ninety automobiles. Today the tower's Promenade serves as a setting for registration, coffee breaks, or bar service for ballroom events.

Over the years the Brown Palace has also been linked—if only in people's minds—with another building across Tremont Place: the old Navarre, now a private office building. Originally built as the Brinker Collegiate Institute and opened in 1880, the Navarre, also designed by Frank Edbrooke, housed young ladies intent on learning the "fineries" of life. Later the college fell into the hands of a pair of gamblers, C. W. Hunsicker and Bob Stockton, who called it the Richelieu. They lost it, gambling, to Vasto Chucovich and Ed Chace.

The new gambling pair named it for Henry of Navarre, a lover of wine, women, and song—the very reasons for which their business existed—and it became the residence for quite another class of young women. At this time, the early 1900s, stories began to circulate of a mysterious tunnel with a rail line by which gentlemen who might be inconveniently recognized could come and go from the Navarre unseen by the gossips.

A local television documentary on tunnels during the 1990s was able to find subterranean tracks at the Navarre end, but the tunnel ended in a brick wall. Efforts to trace its presence under Tremont Place with sophisticated equipment failed to turn up any evidence of a passageway to the Brown Palace. Yet the story has been kept alive by old-time employees who relay it to their juniors. A Ship Tavern captain was told by a former captain that the tunnel was where, during Prohibition, he colored grain alcohol to look like whiskey, a brew allegedly then served in teapots in the Tea Room. Were these memories true, or were they tales concocted to widen the eyes of newcomers? No one really knows.

An artist's rendering of the 1959 expansion, this sketch became the main promotional tool for the Brown Palace in the 1960s. Advertisements touted the six hundred fully air conditioned rooms available in the complex.

Charles O'Toole, general manager of the Brown Palace from 1954 to 1960, and Edgar Britton, a Littleton artist, admire the solid walnut relief carving in the new escalator lobby in November 1958. The lobby also featured a mosaic stone wall and a real waterfall.

Who Has Passed Down These Onyx Halls?

Theodore Roosevelt (1858–1919) was the first U.S. president to stop at the Brown Palace, although he did not stay the night. The hearty Teddy had come to Colorado to hunt bears in the spring of 1905. Following a successful twenty-five days in the country around Glenwood Springs, during which he killed twenty-five bears, he came to Denver by train in May to speak to the city's businessmen at an elaborate banquet at the hotel.

Denver and the Brown Palace went all out to greet the president. A silver eagle, 128 inches tip to tip, adorned the Seventeenth Street entrance along with a large portrait of Roosevelt. Along a flag-lined parade route, residents got a good look at their robust chief. But security for a presidential visit was tight—after all, Roosevelt had come to office after William McKinley's assassination in 1901—and the general public was not admitted above the hotel's fifth floor after he arrived. Six policemen were stationed at each door, and fifteen uniformed officers, numerous detectives, and Secret Service personnel kept watch on the eighth floor, where Roosevelt's suite (later known as the Presidential Suite) was located.

The hotel was lavishly decorated in honor of Roosevelt's visit. The *Daily News* described the effect of one thousand American Beauty roses, two thousand pink carnations, and carloads of apple blossoms brought in from orchards near Golden, all of which were estimated to cost $1,000. "Perfume such as might have wafted from that early garden on the day when creation was finished and all things were pronounced 'good,' pervaded every nook and corner of the eighth floor," wrote the enthusiastic reporter. Paintings of the Wild West by J. D. How-

land, which were usually displayed in the bar, decorated the suite.

Following a brief rest, Roosevelt met the members of the Denver Press Club and was made an honorary member. And then a lavish banquet in the eighth-floor ballroom was served by eighty waiters, thirty wine stewards, and thirty cooks and carvers. The guests, who paid $10 a plate to attend, consumed five hundred quarts of champagne and 1,500 "fragrant cigars." The estimated cost of the food and service was $4,750.

An orchestra played the popular tunes of the day, from "In the Good Old Summer Time" to "There'll Be a Hot Time in the Old Town Tonight." It was reported that "Hot Time" so delighted the jovial Teddy that he banged his palms on the table and led the singing. "[T]he director of the evening's entertainment," wrote the *Daily News* reporter the next day, "thought the dignity of the occasion was being lost sight of, and demanded a different class of musical interlude." However, the grande finale was still the merry "We Won't Go Home until Morning."

Long speeches followed the dinner, the guests turned the 1,500 cigars into ashes, and at the end of the gala Teddy was escorted to Union Station and waved off to Chicago in his private railroad car.

For all the grandeur, merriment, and adoration, what T. R. remembered most, according to his book *Outdoor Pastimes of an American Hunter* (1905) were "the pretty, musical house finches, to the exclusion of the ordinary city sparrows. . . . It was delightful to hear the males singing, often on the wing. They went right up to the top stories of the high hotel, and nested under the eaves and cornices."

Following President Theodore Roosevelt's visit to the Brown Palace in 1905, this corner room on the eighth floor (opposite top left and right) became known as the Presidential Suite. In 1912, while campaigning for reelection on the Bull Moose Party ticket, Roosevelt returned to the Brown Palace (right). After the renovation of the eighth and ninth floors in 2000, a newly designed suite named in Roosevelt's honor opened on the ninth floor (opposite bottom).

Many people confuse the Brown who built the hotel with the Brown who married the famous "Unsinkable Molly." Although it is said that Margaret "Molly" Tobin Brown (1867–1932) often passed herself off as the wife of "Leadville Johnny" Campion rather than James J. Brown, no record remains to indicate that she was identified with Henry C. Brown.

Returning home to Denver following the *Titanic* disaster, Mrs. Brown checked into the Brown Palace on April 29, 1912—her signature appears in the guest register for that date—and received the media in her hotel apartments. A *Rocky Mountain News* reporter quoted her as saying, "... a tragedy like that of the *Titanic* ... was as unnecessary as running the Brown Palace into Pikes Peak...."

Indeed, Molly Brown was fond of the Brown Palace and frequently took up residence there when her own home at 1340 Pennsylvania Street was rented out. According to Charles O'Toole, the former general manager, Room 629 was always reserved for her. A bellboy during the 1930s, when she stayed at the hotel, he remembered the remarkable lady well. "She always had ambitions to be a person of the theatre," O'Toole recalled in 1960 to Pasquale Marranzino, a *Rocky Mountain*

News columnist. "She recited poetry, tried to learn acting under Sarah Bernhardt, and took singing lessons."

It was the singing lessons that stirred up the Brown Palace. Her singing coach would arrive daily at 10 a.m. with his portmanteau, and soon after "the most awful bellowing would issue from her room." Other guests would complain, but everyone was afraid of Mrs. Brown, who carried a tall duchess's cane and was not above using it to discipline those who displeased her.

"But she was gentle, too," O'Toole remembered. "At Christmas, she had a small tree decorated and placed on the lobby registration desk. Then, the maids, porters, bellhops, waiters and cooks would line up and Mrs. Brown would present each with a gift."

In 1927 Molly Brown entertained royalty in the hotel's Presidential Suite. Princess Stephanie Dolgorouky, descendant of the earliest Russian czars and a cousin of Queen Marie of Romania, traveled to Denver to visit her longtime friend Mrs. Brown. After the train pulled into station, however, Princess Stephanie could not be found. Mrs. Brown led a car-by-car search for Her Highness. Just as she was about to give up, she saw the princess step out of a baggage car. Unaware that a redcap was standing by to retrieve her luggage, the princess had collected her own.

The fashionable Mrs. James J. Brown (opposite)—the intrepid Molly of *Titanic* fame—was no relation to Henry C. Brown, founder of the Brown Palace. However, she often took up residence in the Brown Palace, even though she had an imposing Queen Anne–style house (1890) on Capitol Hill (above left), designed by William Lang. A plan to demolish her house spurred the creation of Historic Denver, Inc. The house was saved and today is open to visitors. This prominent woman needed only to sign as "Mrs. Brown" in the hotel register (above right) to announce her arrival.

Honeymooners from around the world seek accommodations at the Brown Palace, but not all love affairs at the hotel have had happy endings.

The unfortunate Mrs. Isabelle "Sassy" Springer, who in 1911 was the direct cause of the first murder to take place in the hotel, was perhaps a little too romantic. She was carrying on affairs with two gentlemen while still living with her husband, John W. Springer. One of her lovers, Louis Von Phul, a wine salesman, had already had two of his front teeth shot out by a jealous husband. So he was not particularly concerned by the threats made by Mrs. Springer's other lover, Harold Frank Henwood.

On May 24, 1911, *The Follies of 1910* opened at the Broadway Theater across the street from the Brown Palace. After the play Von Phul invited a few gentlemen to join him at the popular men's bar in the Brown Palace. Henwood was already at the bar when Von Phul's party arrived. Insults had been exchanged earlier, and Henwood was carrying a gun under his coat. When he saw Von Phul and his friends, he made a few suggestive remarks to the wine salesman. Von Phul excused himself, walked up to Henwood, and knocked him to the floor. Dusting his hands as if to put a finish to the unpleasant incident, he rejoined his party.

Unfortunately, the fight was not over. Henwood fumbled for the gun from beneath his coat and, before anyone realized what was happening, fired five rapid shots, three of which struck Von Phul. A member of the bar orchestra—Paul Whiteman, a Denver boy who became one of the great band leaders of the Big Band era—grabbed a handkerchief from Von Phul's pocket and tried to stop the bleeding. Von Phul was rushed to the hospital, where he died that night.

The Springers were subsequently divorced, and Sassy

Springer left town only to become embroiled in other unsavory love affairs in the East. Henwood died in prison eighteen years later, kept alive only through legal maneuvers that stayed his sentence of hanging.

Another romance paired Jane Tomberlin, a divorced Denver socialite, and Samuel Crowingburg-Amalu, a descendant of Hawaiian kings. They met in an elevator at the Brown Palace—and it was love at first *aloha*. Within days, they had set the wedding date and made plans for a ceremony and lavish reception at the hotel. Thus began a saga in which the groom failed to appear and then claimed that he was kidnapped, after which the couple were married at the Antlers Hotel in Colorado Springs. A week later the prince was in jail, facing charges that he had written bad checks at both the Brown and the Antlers. At first Jane threatened annulment, but Sam wooed her again. She vowed to stand by him, even though he and members of his entourage were indicted on interstate transportation of forged securities, cashing worthless checks, and scheming to defraud various hotels, including the Brown Palace. The Brown brought suit for $2,066.83, an amount that allegedly led Sam to comment: "I can't understand what the 83 cents is for." At the close of the trial's first day, Sam and Jane relaxed over wine in the Ship Tavern. But after the prince was sentenced to four years in federal prison for fraud, Jane filed for a divorce in Honolulu and disappeared from the Denver newspapers. Sam was later picked up in Oregon for violating his parole. Along the way he had stopped off in Dallas, where he owed a hotel an even $1,800.

Many actors who performed at the opulent Broadway Theater (1890) (opposite), designed by Frank Edbrooke, stayed at the Brown Palace, which was just across the street. On May 24, 1911, several Brown Palace guests took in a show at the theater and then retired to their hotel rooms. That night the popular men's bar (above) became the scene of a sensational murder.

In 1932 Franklin D. Roosevelt (1882–1945), then governor of New York State and the Democratic Party's nominee for president, visited the Brown Palace. Arriving at Denver's Union Station on September 15, Roosevelt was greeted by William H. Adams, governor of Colorado, and escorted along a parade route to the Brown Palace, where thousands of people awaited his arrival. Those inside the hotel heard the presidential candidate's brief speech from the second-floor balcony. Later, seated in a plush armchair in the Presidential Suite, Roosevelt conducted press interviews. That evening he hosted an informal dinner for women members of the state's Democratic Party.

One woman who stayed at the hotel during Roosevelt's visit remembered that the elevator was blocked off for the presidential candidate. Nevertheless, she had pushed the button on her floor, and when the elevator stopped, with Roosevelt in it, the governor's security detail tried to turn her away. Roosevelt welcomed her, however, and she rode down with the candidate.

Denver had a reputation of being a "serviceman's town" during World War II. Many Army and Navy Club hostesses danced with soldiers and fell in love at the hotel. One woman recalls dancing with a soldier from Europe who had lost his whole family in the Holocaust. "For one night, the Brown Palace provided the perfect escape for those memories," she later wrote.

On another occasion a group of pilots ferrying planes to an airfield in the Midwest became caught in a blizzard and found themselves snowbound in Denver. They found accommodations at the Brown Palace, where an elderly desk clerk reminded them not to knock things around in their room because one wall was completely mirrored. The young pilots, having a night off, had no intention of hanging around in a hotel room and set out to celebrate their break in routine. One man, however, celebrated too quickly and too much. His companions took him back to the hotel, put him to bed, and went out again. When they returned, "There was the unmistakable smell of gunpowder [and] a bullet hole in the mirror." Their companion had awakened from his stupor and, as he staggered to the bathroom, saw an unrecognizable shape in the mirror. Thinking that he had surprised an intruder, he grabbed his gun, fired a shot, and fell back into bed.

By 1932, when Theodore Roosevelt's cousin Franklin visited the Brown Palace, the Presidential Suite (above left) had taken on a new elegance. Among the numerous guests FDR received in his suite (above right) were Alva B. Adams, the Democratic nominee for the U.S. Senate, and Democratic Senator Edward P. Costigan.

The Brown Palace did its share to support the American effort during World War II. A V-shaped table displays the result of its participation in the victory garden campaign—more than six hundred cans of Colorado-grown fruit and vegetables—while the staff gives the victory salute (opposite top). Activities in the lobby included a salute to Army Air Force Day and a dinner for bond purchasers (opposite bottom left and right).

BROWN PALACE HOTEL
featuring
Colorado
Fruits And Vegetables

Although numerous presidents have visited and stayed overnight at the Brown Palace, the hotel was a home for Dwight D. Eisenhower. Mamie Doud had grown up in her parents' Lafayette Street house in Denver's Capitol Hill area, and Mamie and Ike were considered home-town folks. When Ike became a candidate for president in 1952, the Brown Palace became his preconvention head-quarters. The staff took the Eisenhowers into their hearts.

At that time, as a candidate, Ike did not have the staff to handle the great volume of foreign mail that poured into his headquarters. Thousands of letters arrived, many written in the writers' native language. When the hotel staff learned of the deluge of letters, they orga-nized a voluntary band of interpreters, drawing on the twenty or so foreign languages spoken and read among them. After the Palace Arms, the most formal of the hotel's dining rooms, closed for the night, the volunteers gathered at the undressed tables and worked far into the night, translating the requests and messages of good will that came to the general from people around the world who loved and admired him for his role in lead-ing the American and European forces to victory in World War II.

As president and first lady, Ike and Mamie often vaca-tioned in Mile-High City, and during these visits the Brown Palace always served as the Western White House. While there, Ike loved to fish and play golf. In fact, the president occasionally practiced his golf swing in the living room of his hotel suite. On one occasion an errant golf ball left a dent in the fireplace mantel, a reminder of the years when the Brown Palace served as the Western White House.

One day, following a few rounds of golf, President Eisenhower invited a group of friends to dinner at the hotel. Executive Chef Ira Dole, who was solely respon-sible for preparing the president's meals, decided to cre-ate a special dish for the occasion. Beef Tenderloin à la Presidente so pleased Ike that he ordered it three days in a row. For another Eisenhower dinner, the staff pro-duced an ice carving of a mountain, complete with lit-tle pine trees and at its base a miniature lake, in which three tiny trout swam.

Dole began working in hotel kitchens at the age of fifteen, washing pots and pans at the Broadmoor Hotel in Colorado Springs. He advanced through the ranks, preparing vegetables and pastries, learning about aging and cutting meat, broiling and frying. When he came to the Brown Palace in 1941, he began as a fry cook and then progressed to second cook, sous chef, and finally executive chef.

One of Dole's favorite stories about Ike might have had a tragic ending. One day when the two went fishing, the president's line somehow became entangled in some debris midstream. Trying to pull it free, Ike almost slipped into the river. Dole's sturdy arm pulled the most powerful man in the world back to safety.

67

The Eisenhowers turned the Brown Palace's Presidential Suite into a home. The 2000 renovations created an official White House look for the hotel's most treasured suite (opposite top).

Chef Ira Dole (opposite bottom left), who retired in 1982 after forty-one years at the Brown Palace, was the longest-reigning executive chef in the country. His ice-sculpture lake stocked with live trout was such a hit that replicas were made into the 1960s (opposite bottom right). When one trout suddenly flipped out of the icy pool, the president leaped out of his chair to the rescue, nearly upsetting the table.

Ike joined in the fun at a children's party at the Brown Palace hosted by the American Legion (right).

Royal guests at the Brown Palace have ranged from impecunious younger sons of fading dynasties to oil-rich sheiks with their entourages. Beginning in 1916, Frank Setvin, the hotel's catering manager, kept a record of such famous visitors. He also purchased a small American flag to decorate the banquet table set for William Jennings Bryan following his resignation as secretary of state. Thereafter the flag was used on every banquet table at which VIPs sat. When he retired, Setvin took the flag, framed it, and created a hand-lettered plaque to go with it, listing the names of all those who had sat at tables with the flag. The flag and plaque were donated to the hotel in 1980 by Setvin's daughter.

Shortly after the Brown Palace opened, in the waning years of the nineteenth century, young Count Koenigsmarche of Germany came to Denver. He had been forced to leave home because of some disastrous youthful prank, the details of which were not reported in the Denver papers. Although he had plenty of money when he arrived, he lived high and eventually found himself in financial straits. Being a resourceful young man, Count Koenigsmarche did not write home for more money. Instead he went to work at the Brown Palace as a bookkeeper and served diligently until at last his father sent word that all the fuss at home had been smoothed over and that it was safe for him to return to Germany.

Still another count, this one from Russia, worked at

the Brown Palace a few years later. He was a barber by trade, and it was claimed that he had shaved President William McKinley (but apparently not at the Brown Palace). Unlike Koenigsmarche, this count did not fare well in America. Later news stories reported that he got in trouble in Omaha for forging checks.

Dr. Sun Yat-Sen (1866–1925), the founding father of the Republic of China, visited Denver in 1911 to raise funds for the overthrow of the Ch'ing Dynasty. According to the September 1942 issue of *Colorado Magazine*, "A small, dark, bespectacled man stood on the stage of the old Chinese Theater on Market Street and made an impassioned plea for funds to help free his countrymen." News of the start of the revolution—the revolutionary forces' seizing of the government munitions depot in Wuchang, China—reached Dr. Sun in Denver on October 10 while he was staying in Room 321 of the Brown Palace. On that historic day the Chinese residents of Denver raised $500 for the revolution. Later that year Dr. Sun returned to his country, where he was elected provisional president of the Republic of China and assumed office on January 1, 1912, in Nanking.

When Queen Marie of Romania visited Denver in 1926, she was accorded the ultimate red-carpet treatment during her stay at the Brown Palace. A special door was made so that she could walk directly from her limousine to the elevators without having to come in contact with the common folk who came to gawk at royal visitors. Other royal guests who came to Denver to stay at the Brown Palace and mingle with the city's social lions at banquets have included Prince William, the crown prince of Sweden, on October 19, 1927, and Prince Frederik and Princess Ingrid, the crown prince and princess of Denmark and Iceland, on April 17, 1939. More recent royal visitors have included the United Kingdom's Princess Anne on June 17, 1983, and Emperor Akihito and Empress Michiko of Japan on June 20, 1994.

The Brown Palace guest register for October 10, 1911 (left), shows that Dr. Sun Yat-Sen and his associate W. S. Wong were the last guests to register that day. Brown Palace style sets the tone when the hotel entertains royalty (opposite). Lavish banquets were held in honor of Queen Marie of Romania in 1926 (top left); HRH Prince William of Sweden in 1927, as this dinner brochure indicates (middle left); and Prince Frederik and Princess Ingrid, the crown prince and princess of Denmark and Iceland, in 1939 (top right). The United Kingdom's Princess Anne visited in 1983 (bottom right). Managing Director Armel Santens and his wife, Elisabeth, greeted President George W. Bush at Ellyngton's in August 2001 (bottom left).

MILE HIGH CLUB

Supper

at the

BROWN PALACE HOTEL

DENVER

WEDNESDAY, OCTOBER THE NINETEENTH

Nineteen hundred and twenty-seven

H. R. H. PRINCE WILLIAM OF SWEDEN

Guest of Honor

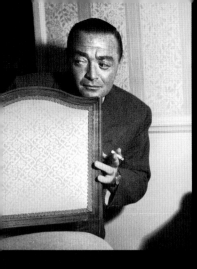

Since the 1890s, when names such as Lionel Barrymore and John Philip Sousa graced the pages of the Brown Palace register, the hotel has welcomed celebrated guests. Here is a glimpse of some glamorous visitors inside their guest rooms, courtesy of Bill Peery, a former *Rocky Mountain News* photographer. In 1962 Peter Lorre (opposite top left) came to Denver for the premier of his film *Five Weeks in a Balloon*. The sophisticated Jane Russell (opposite middle left) strikes a stylish pose. Robert Taylor and wife (opposite bottom left) enjoy a quiet moment together. The incomparable George Jessel relaxes (opposite bottom right). Red Skelton (opposite top right) painted this "self-portrait" in his guest room in 1977. John Wayne (top right) strode into Denver in August 1960 for the world premier of his film *The Alamo*. Helen Hayes (top left), the "First Lady of American Theater," unwinds during a busy trip in 1963. Jimmy Durante (left)—"The Schnozz"—presents a young fan with a gift in the Presidential Suite.

Ringo Starr arrives at the Brown Palace's Broadway service entrance in August 1964 and is whisked up to his eighth-floor suite. More than three decades later he returned to Denver and the Brown Palace, once again occupying the Beatles Suite while in town to play a concert at Red Rocks Amphitheater.

Nothing that happened at the Brown Palace from its opening in 1892 could compare with the one-night visit of the Beatles in 1964. The hotel was not particularly keen on hosting the English rock group for its Denver appearance at Red Rocks Amphitheater, but the Beatles' manager would not accept no for an answer: the Beatles *had* to stay at the Brown Palace. Reluctantly, the hotel acquiesced, and the city and the hotel took advice offered by other cities where the group had appeared about how to deal with this cultural phenomenon.

Days before the Beatles were due to arrive, the hotel was besieged by people who used any excuse to make contact with the young men. Girls as young as twelve and thirteen came to the employment office seeking jobs as maids in the hope that they might get a glimpse of their idols and even get to touch items the Beatles used. Other people wanted to bring in cakes and other homemade sweets to show their love. Still others made offers to buy the sheets the Fab Four slept on—unwashed, of course.

Although the group's plane was not scheduled to arrive until midafternoon, crowds of young girls congregated outside the hotel by early morning. At zero hour the police, who were trying to keep things under control, estimated the crowd at more than five thousand teenagers. Adults, possibly afraid of being crushed, flocked to the roofs of nearby buildings or stood well out of the way on fire escapes.

Even before the four Brits arrived, girls fainted and had to be carried into the Brown Palace lobby to be revived. Some were trampled where they fell and had to be taken to the hospital. Small children were separated from older siblings, and a lost child center was set up in a corner of the lobby. One patrolman was bitten on the finger, another elbowed in the face, losing a false tooth in the action. Altogether seven people were hospitalized, a small number compared with the casualties in other cities.

When the Beatles finally arrived, however, almost no one in the assembled crowd saw them. They slipped into the hotel by a service entrance and reached their floor by a service elevator.

A room service waiter recalled his encounter with the young musicians. The group placed an order for grilled cheese sandwiches and chips. When the waiter delivered the sandwich order—accompanied by potato chips, not the English-style french fries—he heard the young men exclaim, "Bloody Americans and their chips with everything!"

73

Usually the Brown Palace hosts presidents, other heads of state, and visiting royalty one at a time. But the prestigious Summit of the Eight held in Denver on June 20–22, 1997, involved not only the host, U.S. President Bill Clinton, but also leaders from other industrialized nations: Russian President Boris Yeltsin, French President Jacques Chirac, Italian Prime Minister Romano Prodi, Canadian Prime Minister Jean Chretien, British Prime Minister Tony Blair, Japanese Prime Minister Ryutaro Hashimoto, and German Chancellor Helmut Kohl. The U.S. delegation included President and Mrs. Clinton, Secretary of State Madeleine Albright, and Secretary of the Treasury Robert Rubin. In addition to staying at the Brown Palace, the visiting dignitaries, spouses, and senior staff would be dining in the hotel's restaurants.

Of course, a president does not simply arrive at a hotel's front desk and ask for a room. His security and protocol assistants fly in as early as a month before the event to inspect the facilities and discuss matters with management and hotel security personnel.

Ten days before President Clinton checked in, the White House communication agency staff arrived with three big trucks filled with equipment, which was installed in staff meeting rooms and an office on the rooftop floor. The installation required running hundreds of feet of power cables, network wires, and coaxial cable. A second communications center was set up on the eighth floor. So efficient was this operation that anyone who called the White House in Washington, D.C., was instantly routed through the hotel's switchboard and the call was answered, "White House, Denver."

Security precautions were very different from the 1950s, when President Eisenhower used the lobby entrance to enter and exit the hotel with only a small contingent of Secret Service personnel. For the Summit of the Eight, the three streets around the Brown Palace were blocked off; a custom-made white fabric tunnel shielded access from the curb to the front steps, and blue fabric drapes installed between the lobby and the elevators were drawn whenever the president or first lady entered or departed.

Twenty-one hotel rooms were stripped of furniture and converted into working offices for the secretary of state, secretary of the treasury, National Security Council, and first lady. More than three hundred computers and printers, twenty-four fax machines, and thirty copiers were brought from Washington for use in these offices.

Two White House stewards came to Denver to oversee preparation of the first family's food. The hotel's full-time upholsterer recovered two love seats for the president's room. When the Brown Palace flower shop manager learned that President Clinton was allergic to fresh flowers, she prepared silk flower arrangements for his room.

Before President Clinton met with President Yeltsin, White House aides asked the hotel's pianist and harpist, who accompany afternoon tea in the lobby, to play while the two presidents posed for photographs on the mezzanine above the grand staircase. With only fifteen minutes to prepare, John Kite, the pianist, and Nancy Brace, the harpist, decided on a piece from Clinton's Inauguration ceremony—Aaron Copland's "Simple Gifts" from *Appalachian Spring,* one of the president's favorite pieces. President Clinton was deeply moved by the gesture.

When the hotel staff began putting the house in order again on the following Monday, the dramatic Summit of the Eight took its place as another piece of Brown Palace history.

74

The Gold Room (left), as planned by C. Ed Stanton in 1955, featured monochromatic tones of gold and walnut with walls painted in gold leaf. The room, located on the second floor, became the "Oval Office" for President Bill Clinton during the Summit of the Eight in June 1997. Originally a G7 economic conference, it evolved into the Summit of the Eight when President Clinton invited Russian President Boris Yeltsin to attend. The two leaders greeted the public from the second-floor balcony overlooking the Brown Palace's atrium lobby (opposite).

From the actress Anna Held's dog, who did not stay, to Zsa Zsa Gabor's kitten, who stayed longer than Zsa Zsa did, four-footed companions have contributed their own antics to the Brown Palace's story. The first to leave her imprint—literally—was Lizzie, the hotel's cat. Legend has it that when the hotel was under construction, she strolled through the wet cement, forever preserving her paw prints in one of the basement's many storage rooms. Once, while walking along the eighth-floor railing, she lost her footing and fell to the lobby below, landing on her feet in proper cat fashion but startling the prominent guests gathered there.

The first dog known to have stayed in the Brown Palace was a fox terrier from Philadelphia that had been willed $50,000 by his late master. When the man lay dying, the dog allegedly would neither eat nor sleep and became consumptive. Just as doctors of the period sent tuberculosis patients to the West to recover, a veterinarian prescribed a sojourn in the Rocky Mountain air. In 1896, four years after the Brown Palace opened, the wealthy, ailing pooch—accompanied by two daughters of his late master, a gentleman friend of the family, and a nursemaid—took a suite of seven rooms on the hotel's second floor. The records do not reveal whether or not he recovered.

A few years later, the hotel's dog policy had apparently changed. When Anna Held and her husband, the theater producer Florence Ziegfeld, attempted to register with her small French poodle, Blackie, they were refused. Even a bribe offered to the desk clerk failed, although such tactics had always worked at the Waldorf-Astoria and other elegant hotels. Luckily, the Ziegfelds could retreat to their private railroad car, "Starlight," where Blackie undoubtedly felt more at home.

In 1896 Brown Palace guests were awakened about 1 A.M., the *Chicago Times Herald* reported, by "the loud and somewhat truculent song of a rooster . . . reverberating through the corridors and down the marble stairways. . . ." When at 2 A.M. the clarion sounded again, bellboys traced the sound to the room of Lord Ogilvie, a frequent English visitor. The clerk was summoned. At his knock, the lord awoke and beckoned the clerk to come in. "On the head of the Englishman's bed was perched a fine brass-backed game, the winner of a hundred battles and the owner of a voice like a bugle. He regarded the strangers with a hostile eye and crowed again." The clerk explained that pets were not allowed in the rooms and that one of the bellboys must remove the rooster. "Not in a thousand years, not in ten centuries. This is not a pet. This is an alarm clock. The last time I was here, you let me miss a train and this time, I've brought something I can rely on to call me at 6:00 o'clock. It's all right. Adios; good night." The *Denver Times*, however, maintained that Ogilvie himself "could crow like a rooster and did so whenever there was too much noise going on." Lord Ogilvie later renounced his title, married a Colorado girl, and became a solid, if still eccentric, citizen.

Perhaps no animal has caused so much consternation as a very adventurous kitten, one of a pair given to the actress Zsa Zsa Gabor during a Denver visit in 1970. As she checked out to make connections for her next personal appearance, the kitten was missing, although its cries could be heard from within the walls near her room. With instructions to "Ship it to me, Dahling," Miss Gabor gathered up its mate and departed. Having determined that the kitten had crawled under a register and into a hollow terra-cotta block, the hotel staff sent for some sardines from the kitchen. The kitten followed its nose through the maze, into the arms of a much-relieved assistant manager.

7 7

The Brown Palace's furry guests through the years have strolled along the cast-iron balcony railings, explored the ventilation system, and stood on the mantel of the lobby fireplace (opposite). Some four-legged friends have been served dinner on Brown Palace china while seated on the sidewalk outside the hotel, while others have taken up residence in the sandstone walls. Interspersed among the hotel's seventh-story windows are twenty-six stone medallions with carvings of native Rocky Mountain fauna (insets), created by the Denver artist James Whitehouse.

Founded in 1906, fourteen years after the hotel itself, the National Western Stock Show and Rodeo, held in January, has had a long and sometimes curious association with the Brown Palace. As a first-time guest at the hotel in 1945 recalled, "We were from Iowa, and my mother and I had been told we should certainly stay at the Brown Palace for it was the finest hotel in Denver. Well, we came into the lobby and almost turned and walked out. What kind of a hotel, we asked ourselves, would keep cattle in its lobby!" The cattle on display—an event photographed for *Life* magazine—were two prize-winning bulls owned by Dan Thornton, who later served as governor of Colorado, from 1951 to 1955.

A decade later, one Cadillac-mounted visitor from Gunnison taught the city slickers a parking lesson when he dropped in. "The Stetsoned rancher," reported the *Rocky Mountain News*, "tethered his steed on Broadway, spent the afternoon in the Brown Palace Ship Tavern, and paid stall charges without once moving from his drink." The meter was loose, he explained to curious fellow imbibers, so he simply lifted it from the pole. The visitor punctually dropped in a nickel every hour on the hour. "He left the meter in the Tavern and drove away before anyone got his name," the story noted. A call from the hotel brought police to reclaim the meter.

Startling guests and staff alike in January 1958 was a horse named Rex. He and his rider, the cowboy trick-roper Monte Montana, not only invaded the lobby but actually picked their way up the grand staircase and along the second-floor halls to drop in on the Rodeo Cowboys Association, which was meeting in the Gold Room.

Tales of high living among the cattle barons undoubtedly prompted a Walter Mitty–like cowboy from Platteville, Colorado, in 1960 to represent himself as an employee of a leading stock supplier to the National Western Stock Show and Rodeo. For a month he lived it up at the Brown Palace. When his masquerade was finally revealed, he had run up a bill for $578.90, which was pretty big money in 1960.

A year earlier some Texans who grew tired of waiting for service in the hotel's San Marco Room behaved in typical stock show fashion even though the show had not yet opened. William J. Barker, in his "Wayward Reporter" column in the *Denver Post*, immortalized the moment: "Party of large Texans—big, fun-loving souls—was kept waiting in the posh, busy showplace. Finally one of 'em (possibly the biggest) arose and headed for a small, normally suave waiter. The latter said hurriedly, 'Your waitress'll be right over, sir.' The Texan said easily, 'I want you instead.' Then he picked up the horrified waiter as you would a child, whopped him a good one on the pants, put him down again and went back to the Lone Star table."

78

On the tenth anniversary of the National Western Stock Show and Rodeo in 1916, the lobby was decorated with banners, horseshoes, and a carriage with horse and driver (left).

In 1945, after being crowned the stock show's grand and reserve grand champions, Dan Thornton's Triumphant Type Hereford Regent and his son Royal Regent were given the red-carpet treatment when they arrived at the Brown Palace, the beginning of an annual tradition (opposite top). Thornton helped give a Colorado welcome to Jack Benny in 1955 (opposite bottom left).

The arrival of Bubba, a Texas Longhorn steer, and his owner and trainer, Gary Henry, at the front desk signalled the opening of the 1988 show (opposite bottom right).

Brown Palace
Style

While other fine hostelries failed to weather the Great Depression in the 1930s, the Brown Palace carried on in the tradition it had established from the beginning. According to one wag, clerks would ask guests if they came "to sleep or to leap" from the building, although records do not indicate that any came to do the latter.

It was still a time when society dressed to go out for dinner on "maid's night out." On Thursdays and Sundays in the silk-hung Casanova Ballroom on the ground floor, Denver's social figures enjoyed seven-course dinners with French service, all for less than $2. Cocktails were an extravagant 40 cents each. The white-gloved waiters, who served everything on silver service, were paid $13.75 a week but often made more than that in tips each night. The off-duty maids and their boyfriends listened to NBC radio broadcasts of musical acts, such as the Mills Brothers and the Larry Funk Orchestra, that originated at the Brown Palace.

The period of Prohibition (1920–33) at the hotel is best chronicled by the story of how Room 939 was put in "solitary confinement." A group of Spanish-American War veterans convening in town in 1929 arranged to have a little party in the room. They contacted a local bootlegger and had some forbidden beverages delivered. Somebody tattled, and federal agents raided the room and put a padlock on the door for one year. No one knows whether the booze was left inside.

The Casanova's elegant draperies burned in May 1935. Luckily, because the fire broke out in the early morning hours, there were no injuries. The room was reopened in September of that year as the New Casanova Room and in 1941 became the Emerald Room, a dinner-show room where the leading performers of the day entertained, among them the Jules Duke Orchestra, Mindy Carson, Kay Thompson and the Williams Brothers, Mary McCarty, Clark Dennis, and Evelyn Knight.

Although the decor changed with each restaurant remodeling, music

remained a constant. When the space became the San Marco Room in 1959, it featured the strolling violinists of the San Marco Strings. In 1986 the restaurant was renamed Ellyngton's and became the hotel's main dining room for breakfast, lunch, and a lavish Sunday brunch. Redecorated in 1996, it retained the name and continued to showcase a jazz trio on Sunday mornings.

One night a night houseman went to investigate sounds coming from the dining room and discovered a quartet of musicians in formal attire practicing on their instruments. It was long past closing time, and the houseman was not amused. "You're not supposed to be in here," he scolded. "It's late, and I need to clean this room." "Oh, don't worry about us," they assured him. "We live here." And then they vanished.

83

It was the middle of the Great Depression, but New Year's Eve 1934 in the Brown Palace's Casanova Room promised to be festive (opposite). With its 1935 remodeling came a new look and a new band (top and right).

The 1935 New Casanova Room (above) was replaced by the Emerald Room (left). Its grand opening took place on Thanksgiving Eve 1941.

In 1959 the Emerald Room was remodeled as the San Marco Room (opposite top left). Its name and decor were derived from the two-thousand-year-old horses atop St. Mark's Cathedral in Venice.

When Ellyngton's was created in the San Marco space in 1984, the pink Tennessee marble dance floor, made from stone removed from the hotel's exterior, remained (opposite top right).

Ellyngton's decor changed again in 1996 (opposite bottom). Notable guests since then have included Colorado Governor Roy Romer.

Behind the Ship Tavern bar (above) sits a model of the yacht *America*, built in 1851 to race in the first contest to establish a world yachting championship, later known as the America's Cup. On race days many Tavern patrons raise a glass in salute to the model. The Tavern's collection of model clipper ships was originally purchased by C. K. Boettcher on a trip to Cape Cod and presented to his wife as a surprise gift. She offered the ships, evidently not her preferred choice for home decoration, as the centerpiece for the new restaurant. Since the repeal of Prohibition in 1934, the Ship Tavern has been anchored at the Brown Palace's Tremont-Broadway corner (opposite left and right).

Visitors are surprised to find a nautical tavern in Denver. The world-famous "Ship" was created in 1934, shortly after the repeal of Prohibition, as a showplace for a collection of clipper models acquired by C. K. Boettcher, the hotel's owner. Located on the ground floor on the Tremont-Broadway corner, it remains almost unchanged from its original decor, making it the oldest dining room in the hotel.

Created from a former tea room, the Tavern was designed by the Denver architecture firm of Fisher and Fisher. Havens-Batchelder, a local interior design firm, was given carte blanche to decorate it. The paneling is solid chestnut, sandblasted to bring out the grain. The Honduras mahogany bar is made of two of the longest pieces of this wood ever cut, joined at an almost invisible zigzag. The mast and "crow's nest" (a lookout on old sailing ships) are Oregon fir, with cast-brass eyes and belaying pins for making ropes fast.

Alan Fisher recalled that the original concept was to create a seaside inn, but a cast-iron pillar in the middle of the room supporting the whole building could not be removed, so it was turned into the crow's nest. Fisher admitted that he did not research the mast and crow's nest, and they may not be recognizable to any ghosts of sailors that may haunt the tavern. Over the years the feature has beckoned cowboys during the National Western Stock Show and Rodeo and other landlubbers to attempt a climb.

The ship models represent a history of sailing from the early sixteenth century to the early twentieth century. Nearly half are of the exciting clipper ships that powered early American commerce. Perhaps the most famous is *The Flying Cloud*, built in 1851 by the noted shipbuilder Donald McKay and positioned in an alcove behind the bar. *Lightning, Sovereign of the Seas,* and *Stag Hound,* also among the Tavern's collection, are other McKay-built ships. Above the Tavern's kitchen door is a model of the *Thomas W. Lawson,* the world's only seven-masted schooner and the largest sailing vessel ever built at the time of its launch in 1902. In 1907, on her last Atlantic crossing, the *Lawson* was driven broadside into the rocks off the Sculy Isles and broke in two. Only the captain and the engineer survived. The room is also lined with paintings of marine subjects, an ancient ship's clock, and a fine pair of Staffordshire Jamaican Rum barrels made in 1830.

When work on the Tavern was complete, C. K. Boettcher asked one of its carpenters to come down to the hotel. The carpenter, who took his young son with him, thought that some detail had been neglected and that he was being called to the hotel to correct it. When the pair arrived at the hotel, Boettcher was behind the bar hosting a grand opening party. He drew a beer. "I want you to have the first beer served in this tavern," he told the workman, "and you to have the first Coke," he said, handing the youngster the distinctively shaped bottle.

Loyal fans of the Ship Tavern will agree with James Boswell, who wrote in his *Life of Samuel Johnson* (1791): "There is nothing which has yet been contrived by man by which so much happiness is produced as by a good tavern or inn."

87

The Brown Palace has maintained its dress code throughout the years, both for guests in the dining rooms and among its employees. One requirement, recently relaxed, was that men wear coats and ties in the dining room. A man wearing a sport shirt but no tie was once turned away from the Palace Arms, the hotel's most formal dining room; based on the Napoleonic theme, it had opened in 1950. Undeterred, he tried again. This time he lacked not only the tie but his shirt as well—apparently in the belief that because they were meant to go together, they might also be meant not to go together. He still was not allowed in.

The most notorious tie incident, however, involved the Rocky Mountain poet Thomas Hornsby Ferril and was well publicized, first in Ferril's own paper, the *Rocky Mountain Herald,* and then by the *Rocky Mountain News* in July 1956. Having made reservations for lunch at the Palace Arms with a couple of publishing friends from New York, the poet, dressed in a "quiet summer shirt" with the top button unbuttoned but decently covered with a coat, was ushered grandly to a table by two attentive waiters. "But," related Ferril, "I turned out to be as naked as Adam in the Garden. . . . [T]he atmosphere of the Palace Arms began to bristle as if a stray Airedale had just come into the dog pound."

He described how the "Master of the dining room sidled up to me and with the stance of Wellington at Waterloo, gave me what I took to be the eye." This august presence slipped a necktie into the poet's hand. "It was a necktie! An abominable necktie! A cheap rayon necktie! A Father's Day clearance sale necktie! A flamboyant necktie of abstract design combining gangrene squid with magenta bars sinister."

"The Master's speech was rather long and tediously interruptive of a sprightly discussion of what was going on in the literary life of New York, Mexico and Hollywood," Ferril continued. "No matter what we tried to say to each other, there was the Master's voice buzzing like a horsefly."

Such persistence won out, of course. Ferril put on the terrible tie but tied it in a hangman's knot. Each member of the party donned dark glasses to protect them from the dreadful colors and autographed the tie. When, lunch finished, Ferril tried to walk out of the dining room with the tie as a keepsake, the maitre d' followed him, pleading with him not to depart with the tie. He had bought it with his own money so that he could provide for those who showed up without proper dress.

The poet surrendered the tie, but the publicity sent the hotel manager on a shopping trip to assure future guests of a better selection of borrowed finery.

The basic attire for banquet servers has not changed since 1913 (left). Guests dining at the Brown Palace are still waited on by tuxedoed and bow-tied servers, but their ranks now include women.

The Napoleonic theme of the Palace Arms (opposite top left and right) is enhanced by the collection of French military band figures on display in the entryway.

A close look at the Palace Arms reveals its history (opposite bottom). The mirrors on the ceiling and walls are from the days when this space was known as the Mirror Room. Later, when it became the Mayfair Room, gold accents were added to the mirrors.

88

The Brown Palace's kitchen has moved from the top floor to the basement, but its chefs continue to create epicurean delights (top and center, left and right). A lavish banquet in 1945 honored Dan

Thornton's grand champion bulls (left bottom), and, for the hotel's centennial in 1992, a special dessert was created in the shape of the hotel (right bottom). The Independence Room (opposite), a private

dining room inside the Palace Arms, features a French wallpaper pattern, "Views of North American Independence," that hangs in the Diplomatic Receiving Room in the White House.

Afternoon tea was such an accepted ritual for ladies from the time the Brown Palace was opened that no one deemed it necessary to preserve any mention of it. The first record dates to 1911, when a specially catered tea was hosted for wives accompanying their spouses to a convention of Colorado bankers.

During Prohibition, a tea room occupied the space later taken over by the Ship Tavern. Unsubstantiated stories are told that another kind of "tea" was brewed in the tunnel rumored to connect the hotel with the old brothel at the Navarre across Tremont Place. If so, the clientele must not have been only women.

In 1986 the tradition of afternoon tea in the atrium lobby was instituted, and the Brown Palace's tea remains the preferred setting for tea in Denver. For young girls it is often their introduction to social manners. Dressed in their frilliest dresses, these young ladies behave with what one later described as "my Brown Palace manners." Sometimes a boy joins in the ritual, scrubbed to a shine, hair tamed, wearing a suit. He may prefer a soda to tea and scorn the dainty sandwiches, but it is fairly certain that he enjoys the pastries.

Adults have shared their own childhood memories of coming to the Brown Palace. For some the ornate lobby, with its stained-glass ceiling, served as the palace of their favorite fairy tales. They pretended that they were royalty, especially as they descended the grand staircase.

During the hotel's centennial celebration in 1992 one woman remembered her little-girl self presenting a bouquet to Charles Lindbergh when he came to Denver in 1927 after his daring flight across the Atlantic. Following his landing at Lowry Field on August 31, 1927, "Lindy" was given a parade through downtown Denver, the likes of which had not been seen since Theodore Roosevelt visited the city two decades earlier. C. K. Boettcher, the hotel's owner, was the parade chairman and arranged for the event to conclude right in front of the Brown Palace, where Lindbergh spent the night.

Childish pranks, such as running across the wool carpeting to generate static electricity and then touching the elevator button to get a tiny shock, stretched the definition of good manners. The writer Cornelia Otis Skinner even confessed that during her stays at the Brown Palace in the early 1900s, when her father performed at Denver's Elitch Theatre, she liked to spit over the balcony because "it made such a nice splat!"

Another Brown Palace "Eloise" came down with scarlet fever while living at the hotel with her parents. A quarantine of the premises was called for, but the hotel could not shut down for the time required. Instead, the child was sequestered in the family suite at the end of a dark hallway. The quarantine sign was discreetly posted where it was not easily noticed, and the elevator nearby was labeled "out of order." It was the most expensive stay the family ever had at any hotel, the father complained, because he and his wife had to take another suite, the daughter had a live-in nurse, and they had their meals sent up. The quarantine lasted a month.

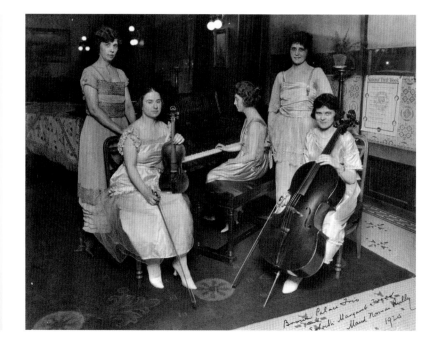

"After the theatre matinee," according to a Brown Palace brochure, "tea in 'The Lounge' at the Brown Palace is the correct thing. No more genteel function has been offered at any hotel." A tea menu from the 1910s (opposite left) lists the offerings. Live music was always provided; this trio and two soloists performed in 1920 (opposite right). The tradition of afternoon tea was reinstated at the Brown Palace in 1986 and given a formal setting in the atrium lobby (above), where it was accompanied by the strains of a harp or piano. Tea was later expanded to include lunch.

Celebrating the holidays at the Brown Palace—beginning with Thanksgiving and lasting through the annual
National Western Stock Show and Rodeo in January—
has long been a tradition for Denver families.

The season kicks off with the Champagne Cascade in
November, a new tradition begun in 1988 to draw attention to the lavish Sunday brunch. In the atrium lobby
employees painstakingly build a
pyramid of six thousand champagne
glasses rising nearly two stories
high, a task that takes almost all day.
The next day the ceremony opens
with the dramatic sabering of bot-
tles of Moët et Chandon champagne. An antique saber neatly
decapitates magnums of the bubbly,
just as was done in the nineteenth
century by Napoleon's victorious
troops. After the sabering ceremony,
an honored employee or guest is
raised by a hydraulic lift to the top of
the gleaming crystal structure to
pour champagne into the topmost
glass. As it overflows into the next
tier and then the next, a sparkling
cascade fills the lobby.

With all the tradition surrounding the Brown
Palace, it is not surprising that even the holiday decorations tell a story. A two-tiered, beaded chandelier
with more than forty-two thousand tiny white lights
intertwined through it, hangs in the center of the
atrium lobby, providing the focus for a winter fantasy-
land theme. This glittering spider chandelier—it has

twelve arms, each adorned with a six-foot beaded
drop, and weighs twenty-five hundred pounds—is
actually a redesigned version of a chandelier that has
hung between the third and fifth floors since the early
1960s. When it is in place, suspended from the roof by
a cable, the lobby is transformed into the enchanted
castle of every child's dream.

Another holiday tradition since
1955 has been the annual Denver
Debutante Ball in December, the
largest party of the year at the
Brown Palace. A benefit for the
Denver Symphony Association, the
ball takes months of planning. The
hotel staff works with the sponsor-
ing debutante ball committee to
plan the dinner menu, wine, music,
and decorations. It is a glamorous
and romantic evening as each debutante, gowned in white, descends
the grand staircase on her father's
arm. She is attended by two escorts,
and her name and antecedents are
announced in carefully practiced
accents, after which she makes her
curtsey to the members of the ball committee and an
atrium full of friends and family. When all the young
women have been presented, they have their first waltz
with their fathers in the atrium under the glittering
chandelier.

For Denver and for the Brown Palace, however, the
holidays are not officially over until the National Western Stock Show and Rodeo closes in late January.

The Champagne Cascade—when champagne flows down a six-thousand-glass,
two-story-high pyramid in the lobby
(above)—officially opens the holiday
season at the Brown Palace.

In a setting of fairy-tale splendor,
Denver society introduces its young
women at the Denver Debutante Ball
(left), held each December at the hotel.

The atrium lobby is dressed for the
holidays from the day after Thanksgiving until late January (opposite).

In 1995 the Brown Palace announced it would be starting an extensive renovation, one that would eventually take seven years to complete and cost almost $20 million. More than just changes in decor, the project involved upgrading technology to provide guests the conveniences of a twenty-first-century hotel. Guest rooms were wired with high-speed Internet access; a full-service business center and a state-of-the-art fitness center were added.

The interior designers for the project drafted plans to highlight the Brown Palace's history and architecture. They enhanced many of the original elements, such as the colors of the atrium's stained glass skylight, which were incorporated in the lobby's specially commissioned carpets and furnishings as well as throughout the second-floor meeting rooms.

Ellyngton's, the restaurant that replaced the San Marco Room, was made to glow with color. Custom-designed wallpaper featured the hotel's emblem: the griffin, a mythical beast that many believe guards the secrets of the business deals made in the popular restaurant. Next door, Henry C.'s Bar became the Churchill Bar, named after the largest cigars manufactured, a room resembling a richly upholstered library. It quickly laid claim to the city's most fashionable cigar lounge, the venue for stories large and small.

Attention turned next to converting the rooms and suites on the top two floors into deluxe state rooms and three presidential suites. In 1937 the eighth and ninth floors had been converted into the Skyline Apartments, and permanent residents were welcomed. Each apartment's decor was "thoroughly modern," following the Art Deco style; for a more residential feel, glass blocks were installed to block the atrium view and the noise. Tenants remained for nearly fifty years, the last one moving out in the mid-1980s.

In 2000, as a tribute to three U.S. presidents who have visited the Brown Palace, three Presidential Suites were created, each decorated to reflect the era of the president for whom it was named. The style of the Eisenhower Suite on the eighth floor, the location of the suite where President Dwight D. Eisenhower stayed, is colonial and Federalist to give it a formal White House look. The Reagan Suite evokes Ronald Reagan's Santa Barbara ranch and his love of western life. The Teddy Roosevelt Suite on the ninth floor is reminiscent of the Edwardian period and features a safari theme.

The Grand Ballroom, Bridge, and Promenade, the venue for many of the city's most prestigious events over the years as well as countless weddings and social affairs, received a facelift in 2002. Graced with crystal chandeliers from the Czech Republic and a ceiling with crown molding, the ballroom still features its original African mahogany paneling, now enhanced with inset lighting and state-of-the-art audio-visual capabilities.

How many stories could the Brown Palace itself tell? Babies were born in the hotel, strangers met and fell in love here, and friends met, quarreled, and parted, never to meet again. Inside its bars, restaurants, and meeting rooms, business deals were made and business deals fell apart. Most of the stories have been forgotten and will never be told. But certainly some of the best stories are yet to be.

97

Redecorated in 2000, the Gold Room (opposite) still features its distinctive royal tones and prominently displays the same gold sunburst clock above the walnut-and-marble fireplace.

A quiet refuge in the bustling hotel, the Churchill Bar (right) allows guests an opportunity to retire to the cordial warmth of this richly appointed room. The space was once the office of Henry C. Brown, founder of the Brown Palace.

98

The Ballroom (opposite top left) provides a formal setting for all business needs, and nearby meeting rooms (opposite top right) offer access to the latest high technology. The Boettcher Board Room (opposite bottom), located on the eighth floor, provides an intimate setting for business meetings and connects to a spacious suite. The Promenade (above) boasts a series of stunning chandeliers made exclusively for the Brown Palace by Preciosa. Workers from the Czech Republic installed the fixtures. Visible to the left is *Lady in Black Hat*, an oil painting in the manner of Thomas Gainsborough, the eighteenth-century English master of portraiture and landscape.

The Reagan Suite (left), with its California Ranch decor, is the latest addition to the Brown's historic Presidential Suites.

Fresh floral arrangements prepared by the Brown Palace's in-house florist (above) add a touch of fragrance and color to the hotel's beauty.

Staterooms on the eighth and ninth floors like this one (opposite) provide modern comforts and technology while honoring the Art Deco tradition of the Skyline Apartments, created in the 1930s.

Well-appointed rooms such as this (above) offer Brown Palace guests the comforts of home, the ease of workplace connectivity, and reminders of the hotel's Victorian origins.

Befitting a palace, a marble-walled bathroom (left), typical of those of the eighth- and ninth-floor staterooms, invites travelers to pamper themselves.

1858. The Denver City Town Company is organized by William H. Larimer Jr.

1860. Henry Cordes Brown arrives in Denver

1863. Brown's carpentry shop becomes home to the Protestant congregation that in 1888 builds Trinity Methodist Church

1864. Brown homesteads in the hills east of town

1867. Brown donates part of his homestead for the Colorado Capitol site

1872. Brown acquires the *Denver Daily* as payment for a debt and runs it for three years

1873. Brown along with C. D. Gurley opens the Bank of Denver in Brown's Tribune Building

1879. Frank E. Edbrooke, the hotel's future architect, arrives in Denver

1889. Brown asks Edbrooke to design his hotel on Seventeenth Street

1892. The Brown Palace Hotel opens on August 12

1894. Brown marries for a third time

1900. Winfield Scott Stratton purchases the mortgage on the hotel

1905. Theodore Roosevelt is the first U.S. president to visit the hotel, inaugurating its Presidential Suite

1906. Brown dies in San Diego at age eighty-five. The National Western Stock Show and Rodeo, which hosts many activities at the hotel over the years, is launched

1908. Stratton's estate buys the hotel

1909. A three-story addition to the hotel is suggested

1910. Myron Stratton Home Corporation takes possession of the hotel

1911. Dr. Sun Yat-sen, on a fund-raising tour of the United States, stays at the Brown Palace

1912–32. The "Unsinkable Molly Brown" (no relation) periodically lives at the Brown Palace

1920. Charles Boettcher, a hardware entrepreneur who had immigrated from Germany, moves into the Brown Palace

1922. Boettcher and Horace W. Bennett buy the hotel

1926. Queen Marie of Romania visits the hotel

1929. Plans are drawn up for a twenty-six-story tower, which is never built

1931. Boettcher and his son, C. K. Boettcher, buy out Bennett's interest in the hotel

1934. The Ship Tavern opens after Prohibition is repealed

1935. Fire damages the Casanova Ballroom; it is remodeled as the New Casanova Room, which was succeeded by the Emerald Room, San Marco Room, and later Ellyngton's

1937. The Skyline Apartments for permanent residents open on the eighth and ninth floors

1948. Charles Boettcher dies

1952. General Dwight D. Eisenhower makes the Brown Palace his preconvention headquarters

1955. The annual Denver Debutante Ball is initiated

1957. Plans for a twenty-two-story tower across Tremont Place are approved; C. K. Boettcher dies

1959. The Tower is built and opens

1963. Charles Boettcher II dies

1964. The Beatles arrive before a concert at Red Rocks Amphitheater

1970. The Brown Palace is added to the National Register of Historic Places

1980. Associated Inns and Restaurants Company of America (AIRCOA) buys and manages the hotel

1983. The hotel is purchased by Integrated Resources

1986. The ritual of afternoon tea is reinstated at the Brown Palace

1987. Management of the hotel is transferred to Rank Hotels of North America

1988. A new tradition, the Champagne Cascade, is launched in the atrium lobby

1989. The hotel is named a Denver landmark

1992. The Brown Palace celebrates its centennial with an outdoor party and other events

1995. Rank Hotels of North America becomes Quorum Hotels and Resorts

1997. The Summit of the Eight brings heads of state to the hotel, including U.S. President Bill Clinton and Russian President Boris Yeltsin

2000. The hotel completes a five-year, $16.5-million restoration

2002. The Grand Ballroom is renovated, marking the hotel's 110th anniversary

The Brown Palace Hotel

ABSOLUTELY FIREPROOF.

❋

THE NEW BROWN HOTEL CO.

Denver, Colo., 4 17 190

Mr. L. C. Woodbury   Room 305

To The New Brown Hotel Co. Dr.

For Room ⁴/10 to ⁴/17	7 days		17	50
Café				80
	Cash 10.00 10.00		20	00
Baggage & Express				
Livery				
Laundry	25	145	1	70
Bar & Wine				
Cigars & Papers				
Telegrams & Messengers				
Baths				
	Valet 100 50		1	50
Bill Rendered				